The Ronald McDonald House of NYC Cookbook

by
the volunteers of The Ronald McDonald
House of New York City

Gryphon III Design Company

Columbus, Ohio

Gryphon III Design Company
364 West First Ave
Columbus, Ohio 43201

© 1994

First Edition
COVER AND INTERIOR DESIGNED BY CATHLEEN CARBERY

Printed in the United States of America

Library of Congress Cataloging-in-Publication Data

The Ronald McDonald House of New York City cookbook/by the
volunteers of the Ronald McDonald House of New York City.

ISBN 0-9642366-0-5

1. Cookery
2. Ronald McDonald House (New York, N.Y.)
I. Ronald McDonald House (New York, N.Y.)

TX714.R633   1994   94-5416
641.5--dc20   CIP

ABOUT OUR HOUSE

New York City's Ronald McDonald House at 405 East 73rd Street offers "a home away from home" for 84 families whose children have cancer.

The Ronald McDonald House, however, is more than just a shelter. It is a special home where families from all over the world can remain united and find comfort and hope during their child's fight with cancer. The medical procedures the children undergo at New York City hospitals may include surgery, radiation therapy, chemotherapy, or bone marrow transplants.

This fight is not made any easier by the harsh economic realities of cancer care. Your donation helps keep the daily cost of a family's stay at the Ronald McDonald House at $20. Other alternatives could cost a family six times the amount, without the comforts of a real home.

All proceeds from the sale of this cookbook help maintain the most supportive and loving environment for these children and their families to call home.

If you would like more information on the Ronald McDonald House of NYC or would like to make an additional donation to the House, please write to us at:

The Ronald McDonald House of NYC
405 E. 73rd Street
New York, NY 10021

For additional copies of this book, please contact us at 212-639-0100.

Thank you for your generous support,

The Ronald McDonald House of NYC

DEDICATION

*To our bubbly
Volunteer Coordinator,
Denise Bomberger,
whose enthusiasm
made this project all
the more enjoyable
and worthwhile.*

ACKNOWLEDGMENTS

For your pleasure and enjoyment, we present these recipes.

This cookbook would not have been possible without the cooperation of our volunteers, staff, board members, and our friends, who gave so generously of their time and agreed to share their favorite recipes. To those of you who submitted recipes, a very big thank you.

Special thanks to House residents Leo Malara and Oleydia Kolkowski. Leo, whose home is in Argentina, contributed some of the food illustrations, and Oleydia, age eleven, who is from Venezuela, drew the illustrations appearing in the collages on the inside covers. This book would also not have been possible without the help of Julie Anderson Tober and Cathleen Carbery, who handled project coordination, design, artwork, and paging pro bono at Gryphon III Design Company in Columbus, Ohio. Our appreciation also goes to dedicated volunteer Betsy Davis, who was the liaison between Julie, Cathleen, and our House.

Thanks also to the volunteer fundraising committee and especially to our cookbook committee, Norma Weiss, Shannon Hubbard, and Pat Ceballos. Special thanks to Daniel Rosenthal, who keyed in all the original recipes.

Simon & Schuster shared the expense of printing the book, and we extend our heartfelt gratitude to President and CEO Jonathan Newcomb, and Amy Nobles, who was the liaison between Simon & Schuster and the House. R.R. Donnelley & Sons contributed their time and expertise by printing the book and its cover, and we are extremely grateful to them.

We do not claim to be a book of solely new and original recipes. Rather, the recipes contained herein are a compilation of our contributors' favorite and successful ventures in the world of cooking. Enjoy!

CONTENTS

Salads and Dressings

Main Dishes

Pastas

Desserts

The Ronald McDonald
House of NYC Cookbook

Hors d'oeuvres
& Appetizers

Crab Melties

Cathy McNulty

Makes 10–15 appetizer servings
Approximately 10 minutes to prepare; 5 minutes to broil

2 jars Old English Cheese (no substitutions)
2 cans "taste of crab" or crabmeat
1-2 pkgs. English muffins
2/3 stick butter or margarine, melted
1/3 c. mayonnaise
garlic salt to taste

Split English muffins and cut the halves into quarters.
Combine all other ingredients and mix well. Spread mixture
onto English muffins (about a teaspoon onto each quarter).
Broil until lightly browned.

Spinach Cheese Squares

Phyllis Light

Makes 40 squares
Bakes for 35 minutes; cools 30 minutes

4 oz. butter
3 eggs
1 c. flour
1 c. milk
1 t. salt
1 t. baking powder
1 lb. Monterey Jack cheese, grated
4 c. chopped spinach

Melt butter in a 9" x 13" pan. Add eggs, flour, milk, salt, and baking powder. Add cheese and spinach; mix well. Spread into pan and bake at 350° for 35 minutes. Cool for 30 minutes and then cut into squares.

Tuna Dip

Christina

Prepare 4 hours before ready to serve

1 lb. can tuna fish, drained
1 8-oz. pkg. cream cheese
1 T lemon juice
2 t. grated onion
1 t. horseradish
1 t. salt

Let cream cheese soften at room temperature for about 2 hours. Then, combine all ingredients until well blended. Refrigerate for about 2 hours prior to serving.

Spinach Party Dip

Tammy Grossman

10-12 minutes to bake

1 round loaf crusty bread
2 (10-oz.) pkgs. chopped spinach
2 (8-oz.) pkgs. cream cheese
1/2 c. chopped onion
3 T. milk   *1 t. lemon juice*
1/2 t. basil   *1/2 t. salt*
1 clove garlic, minced   *1/2 t. pepper*

Preheat oven to 350°. Boil both packages of spinach. Soften cream cheese in a saucepan until it forms a thick liquid. Add all ingredients, except spinach, to cream cheese. Drain spinach and add to cream cheese mixture. Cut out bread so that only the crust is left, with a big hole in the center. Take out center piece of bread to use for dipping, and cut into cubes. Pour cream cheese mixture into center of the bread. Place bread round on a cookie sheet and bake for about 10 to 12 minutes. Serve with cubed bread.

Scandinavian Cucumbers

Norway

Makes 6 servings

1/2 c. sour cream
1 T. sugar
2 T. snipped parsley
1 T. tarragon
1 T. finely chopped onion
1/4 t. dried dill weed
3 small unpared cucumbers, thinly sliced

Stir together all ingredients except cucumbers. Gently fold in cucumbers. Cover and chill 2 hours.

Gravlax (salted salmon)

Nordic Delicacies, Inc.   *Scandinavia*

Makes 12 appetizer servings
20 minutes to prepare; 24 hours to refrigerate

2 lbs. fresh salmon fillet
1/2 c. fresh dill, chopped
1/4 c. salt
1/4 c. sugar
1/4 t. ground white pepper
1/4 t. ground allspice

Rinse salmon and dry with paper towels. Place in a 9" x 13" glass dish. Sprinkle with half of the dill (1/4 cup). In a small bowl, combine salt, sugar, white pepper, allspice. Sprinkle half of mixture over fish and turn fish over. Sprinkle with remaining salt mixture. Top with remaining dill.

Cover with plastic wrap and refrigerate for 24 hours. If a compact texture is desired, place a 7" x 12" dish on top of the fish. Place several cans of food in top dish for weight. Occasionally spoon juices over fish.

To serve, drain fish and cut diagonally in 1/8" slices. Arrange on a platter.

Texas Bean Dip

Wendy Cohen   *United States*

30 minutes to prepare

1/2 lb. ground beef (browned and drained)
1 can refried beans
1 8-oz. can of tomato sauce
1 pkg. taco seasoning mix
1 small onion, finely chopped
1/2 medium green pepper, finely chopped
1/2 t. dry mustard
1/2 t. chili powder
1 c. sour cream
2 T. American cheese
1/4 t. chili powder
lettuce, chopped
taco chips

Mix the first 8 ingredients together and bring to a boil. Mix the next three ingredients together, and pour on top of the first mixture. Sprinkle chopped lettuce and cheese on top. Serve with taco chips.

The Ronald McDonald House of New York City is able to accommodate up to 84 families a day.

Fruit Dip

Ruth Lynch

Makes 4 cups

16 oz. cream cheese, softened
1 large jar marshmallow creme
1 (3-oz.) pkg. strawberry gelatin

Mix all ingredients in bowl. May store in refrigerator for several weeks. Serve with fruit.

Spinach Dip

Greta Michaels

Prepare one day ahead

1 pkg. frozen chopped spinach
1 c. mayonnaise
1 c. sour cream
1 can chopped water chestnuts
1 pkg. leek soup mix

Mix all ingredients well and cool in refrigerator for 24 hours for best results. Especially good dip for fresh vegetables.

Spinach Fritata

Mary Yagaloff

Makes 10–12 servings
45 minutes to bake

3 (10-oz.) pkgs. frozen chopped spinach
4 eggs, beaten
1/4 lb. feta cheese, crumbled
1/4 lb. grated parmesan cheese
1/4 lb. farmer cheese
1/4 lb. pot cheese
pepper to taste

Preheat oven to 375°. Cook spinach until thawed (do not add water). Drain water from spinach.

In a large bowl, mix all ingredients, leaving 1 1/2 T. of grated parmesan for topping. Grease a lasagna-size pan well, including the bottom and sides, with vegetable oil. Spoon mixture into pan and flatten out. Sprinkle top evenly with 1 1/2 T. of grated parmesan (this helps in browning).

Bake at 375° for 45 minutes or until nicely browned on top. When cool, cut into 24 squares.

Quick Pizza Rolls

L. Hanuschak

Makes 4–6 servings
20–25 minutes to bake

1/2 lb. ground beef
1/2 lb. ground spicy hot sausage
1/4 c. onion, chopped
1 clove garlic, chopped
1 T. parsley flakes
1/2 t. basil
celery salt (optional)
1/2 t. oregano
salt and pepper to taste
1 (6-oz.) can tomato paste
1 c. ricotta or cottage cheese
1 egg
1/4 c. grated parmesan cheese
1 pkg. crescent roll dough
6 oz. to 1 lb. mozzarella cheese, thinly sliced

1 T. milk
1 T. sesame seeds

Brown meat and drain off fat. Add onion, garlic, seasonings, and tomato paste. Simmer uncovered for 10 minutes.

Separately combine ricotta or cottage cheese, egg, and parmesan cheese. Set aside.

Unroll crescent dough and separate into 8 rectangles. Place dough on ungreased cookie sheet, overlapping edges to form a rectangle about 15" x 13". Press edges and perforations to seal.

Spread half of meat mixture down the center half of rectangle, leaving a 1" space at the short ends. Top with cheese mixture and spread remaining meat mixture over cheese. Cover with mozzarella slices. Fold short ends of dough over filling, making a 1" border. Then pull long side of dough over filling. Pinch overlapped edges to seal. Brush with milk and sprinkle with sesame seeds.

Bake at 375° for 20 to 25 minutes or until golden brown.

Paté

Andrew Nawn's Mom *France*

2 T. butter
1/3 c. sweet butter
1 large onion, chopped
1 1/2 lbs. chicken livers
1 hard boiled egg
2 T. brandy
1/2 t. salt
dash of pepper

Sauté onion in butter until tender. Add livers to hot, sweet butter. Blend in onion, livers, egg, and brandy until smooth. Season with salt and pepper.

Tomato-Cream Cheese Aspic

Muffy Dent Stuart *United States*

Makes 6–8 servings

2 envelopes gelatin
1/2 c. water
1 can tomato soup
3 (3-oz.) pkgs. cream cheese
1/2 c. chopped olives
1/2 c. chopped celery
1/2 c. chopped onions
1 c. mayonnaise
cottage cheese
cucumbers
lettuce

Soak gelatin in water. Heat soup to a boil and add the gelatin mix. Pour over cheese in a bowl.

Beat the mixture with a mixer. Add vegetables and mayonnaise. Pour into 1-qt. mold. Serve with cottage cheese and cucumbers on lettuce.

Hot Artichoke Dip

Jackie Rusell

45 minutes to bake

1 can artichoke hearts packed in water
1 c. mayonnaise
1 c. grated Italian cheese

Mash artichokes. Add mayonnaise and cheese. Mix all ingredients and sprinkle cheese on top. Bake in 350° oven for 45 minutes.

Curry Dip

Muffy Dent Stuart　　　*United States*

Makes one pint

1 pt. mayonnaise
3 T. chili sauce
3 t. curry powder
1/4 t. salt
1/4 t. pepper
1 T. garlic powder
1 T. grated onion
1 T. Worcestershire sauce

Mix all ingredients together and chill. Keeps indefinitely in refrigerator. Good on raw vegetables or shrimp.

Soups & Stews

Garlic Soup

Natalie Aronson

Makes 4 servings
45 minutes to prepare

1 medium onion, sliced
10 cloves garlic, finely chopped
4 T. butter
1 t. vegetable oil
1-2 T. fresh parsley, chopped
4 c. water
4 chicken bouillon cubes
4 slices Italian or French bread (optional)
4 slices Swiss cheese
salt and pepper

Sauté onion and garlic in butter and oil until the onion is soft. Do not brown. Add parsley, salt, and pepper. Pour in water and bring to a boil. Add bouillon cubes and simmer covered for 30 minutes. Top with Swiss cheese. Serve with Italian or French bread.

Wild Rice and Turkey Bisque

Maria Lazaro Tetzlaff

Makes 4 servings
45 minutes to prepare

1/4 c. margarine
1 large onion, diced
2 carrots, finely diced
2 celery stalks, finely diced
1/4 c. unsifted, all-purpose flour
2 c. cooked turkey, diced
8 c. chicken or turkey broth
4 c. wild white rice (1 1/2 c. uncooked)
2 c. half-and-half or heavy cream
salt and pepper

Melt butter in a large saucepan over medium heat. Add onions, carrots, celery, and turkey. Sauté 3 minutes or until vegetables have softened. Stir in flour a little bit at a time until blended. Cook for 1 minute.

Gradually add broth, stirring until blended. Bring to a boiling simmer while partially covered for about 10 minutes (or until vegetables are tender).

Stir in rice, 1/2 tsp. salt, and 1/4 tsp. pepper. Add half-and-half over low heat. Continue to heat mixture until hot, but not boiling

Fish Soup

Ricki Levenson

Makes 4-6 servings
10 minutes to mix; 30 minutes to cook

3 T. butter
1 chopped onion
3 cloves garlic, chopped
2 t. curry
3 c. chicken broth
1 c. white wine
1 can (1 lb.) tomatoes
1/2 c. rice
2 lbs. cut-up white fish
Herbs of Provence

Sauté onion and garlic in butter. Add other ingredients, except fish. Simmer for 15 minutes.

Add fish. Simmer an additional 15 minutes. Add more broth if too thick.

Greek Easter Soup
Greece

2 lbs. lamb liver or 1 lung of lamb
3 c. water
1/2 c. butter
4 green onions, finely chopped
1/2 c. dill, finely chopped
1/2 c. parsley, finely chopped
1/2 c. rice
salt and pepper
lamb or chicken broth
Avgolemono (egg lemon sauce)

Wash liver or lung well and simmer in water for 15 minutes. Remove from heat, strain broth, and set broth aside.

Chop liver finely. Cook onions, dill, and parsley in butter with 1 t. salt and a dash of pepper until soft and transparent. Be careful not to brown! Add chopped liver and cook over low heat for 5 minutes, stirring frequently.

Add liver broth and lamb or chicken broth to make 2 quarts of liquid. Bring to a boil and add rice. Reduce heat. Cover and cook until rice is tender. Season to taste. Remove from heat and add liver mixture to rice mixture.

Blend with Avgolemono (egg lemon sauce) and serve.

Dublin Coddle

Ireland

Approximately 1 1/2 hours to prepare

3 c. beef broth
1 pkg. pre-cooked breakfast links or Irish pork sausage,
    cut in half
1 pkg. (8 oz.) sliced bacon, cut into 1" pieces
3 lbs. red potatoes, cut into 1/2" slices
3 carrots, sliced
2 large onions, sliced
1/2 c. parsley flakes

Combine broth, sausage, bacon, and 1 c. of water. Boil for 5 minutes. Remove sausage and bacon. Reserve broth.

In a 6-quart Dutch oven, layer half of the potatoes, carrots, onions, sausage, and bacon. Repeat. Add broth and parsley. Bring to a boil. Reduce heat, cover, and simmer for 1 hour or until vegetables are tender.

Avgolemono
(egg lemon sauce)

Greece

4 eggs (at room temperature)
2 T. cold water
Juice from 1 to 1 1/2 lemons
Small amount of lamb or chicken broth, hot

Separate eggs. Beat egg whites until stiff. Blend in egg yolks, then add water and lemon juice and beat until thick.

With ladle, add a small amount of hot broth to egg mixture, blending quickly. Pour this into Greek Easter soup and stir well. Serve at once.

Zucchini Soup

Ginny Seipt

2 lbs. (7-8 c.) zucchini, with seeds removed
2 T. butter or margarine
2 T. onion or shallots
3 c. chicken broth*
1 t. salt
1 t. curry
1 c. milk or cream

Sauté zucchini, butter, and onions until softened. When cooked, put into a blender with chicken broth, curry, and salt.

One cup of milk or cream may be added. Chill and serve. Or chill base first, then add milk before serving.

*One can chicken broth diluted with 1 can of water, and one square of chicken bouillon diluted with 1 cup of water.

Cream of Zucchini Soup

Millie Dent   *Bermuda*

Makes 4 servings
30 minutes to prepare

1 lb. young zucchini
2 T. butter
2 T. finely chopped shallots
1 clove garlic, minced fine
1 t. curry powder
1/2 c. light cream
1/2 t. salt
1 3/4 c. chicken broth

Scrub zucchini and slice thin. Do not peel.

Heat butter and add zucchini, shallots, and garlic. Cover tightly and simmer about 10 minutes. Shake the pan occasionally and do not let vegetables brown.

Spoon the mixture into electric blender, add remaining ingredients and blend.

Serve hot with croutons, or cold with chives.

Approximately one-third of the financial support needed to operate the House is generously provided by the individual men and women who own and run McDonald's restaurants in NY, NJ, and CT, but most of the funds must be raised through corporate and individual donations.

Pasta-Lentil Soup

1 lb. lentils
12 c. water
olive oil
1/4 c. fresh garlic, diced
1/2 c. scallions, chopped
2 medium yellow onions, diced
5 bay leaves
1/2 c. fresh parsley, chopped
1 1/2 c. diced celery
pork or beef soup bone

oregano
crushed red pepper
spaghetti
salt and black pepper

Soak lentils overnight in cold, salted water. Drain and wash.

Cover bottom of large stockpot with olive oil. Over medium heat, sauté garlic, scallions, onions, bay leaves, and parsley. Add water and soup bone. Bring to a boil. Reduce heat and stir in lentils and spices. Cover and simmer for 2 hours, stirring occasionally. Add small amounts of water to desired consistency; should be fairly thick.

Separately boil spaghetti, broken into 1" pieces; add to soup. Serve with parmesan cheese and fresh ground pepper.

Gronkålsuppe
(green kale soup)

Susanne M. Bronifield   Denmark

1 ham bone
1 large onion, chopped
4 stalks of celery, sliced
6 carrots, diced
1 small head of cabbage, finely cut
1 bunch fresh green kale, cut medium-fine
1/4 c. oatmeal

Cook ham bone, onion, celery, and carrots in water. Cover until almost done. Add cabbage and kale, cook 20 minutes. Gradually add oatmeal and cook 10 minutes longer.

Indian Cauliflower Stew

India

Makes 4-6 servings
30 minutes to prepare; 35 minutes to cook

1/4 c. peanut oil
4 cloves garlic, minced
3 T. ginger, chopped
1 small onion, thinly sliced
1/2 t. ground tumeric
1 small cauliflower (about 1 lb.), cut into 1" pieces
2 c. broccoli florets, cut about 1 1/2" long
1 medium tomato, coarsely chopped
2/3 c. vegetable stock, or water
2 T. dry sherry (optional)
2 t. soy sauce, or to taste
1 (10.5-oz.) pkg. of firm tofu, drained and cut into 1" cubes

In a 5-quart microwaveable casserole, combine oil, garlic, ginger, onion, and tumeric.

Microwave on high for 2 minutes. Add cauliflower and stir well to coat with oil. Microwave on high for 6 minutes. Stir in broccoli and microwave on high for 3 minutes.

Add the tomato, stock or water, dry sherry (if desired), and soy sauce. Stir to combine. Cover tightly with lid or vented plastic wrap. Microwave on high for 9 to 14 minutes or until the vegetables are tender, stirring once.

Gently stir in tofu. Re-cover and microwave on high for 1 minute. Let stand, covered, for 10 minutes.

Cream of Asparagus Soup

Linda Huss

Makes 8 to 10 servings
45 minutes to 1 1/2 hours to prepare

1/4 lb. butter
1 large or 2 small leeks, sliced
2 cloves garlic, minced
1/2 c. flour
2 bundles small to medium asparagus (chopped, save tips)
2 large cans College Inn chicken broth
1 pint half-and-half
1/4 t. nutmeg
salt and pepper to taste

Melt butter and sauté leeks and garlic. Add flour and coat leeks completely. Salt and pepper lightly. Add broth and chopped asparagus stalks (steam tips separately and save). Simmer broth mixture 30 minutes to 1 hour. Let cool and put through a blender to purcé. Return to heat. Add asparagus tips and half-and-half. Heat through. Sprinkle with nutmeg.

Summer Fruit Gazpacho

Suki

Makes 25 cups

1 qt. strawberry puree
6 c. orange juice
2 T. sugar
3 T. orange zest
3 T. lemon or lime zest
1 qt. diced cantaloupe
1 qt. diced honeydew melon
2 mangos or papayas, diced
2 apples, peeled and diced
2 c. blueberries
2 c. green or red seedless grapes, halved
kiwi or strawberry slices to garnish

Use ripe strawberries. Pureé in blender. Make a day ahead and refrigerate.

Combine strawberry pureé, orange juice, sugar, orange and lemon zests, cantaloupe, honeydew, and mango in a large bowl. Process half of mixture in a food processor fitted with a steel blade or blend in a blender until smooth. Stir the pureé into the remaining fruit mixture.

Stir in the apples, blueberries, and grapes. Refrigerate covered for several hours.

Ladle the soup into bowls. Top with a dab of sour cream. Garnish with kiwi or strawberries.

Louisiana Beef Stew

Linda Huss

Makes 4-6 servings
20 minutes to prepare; simmer for 2 1/2 hours

3 T. flour
1 t. salt
1/2 t. celery salt
1/4 t. garlic salt
1/4 t. pepper
1/2 t. ginger
3 lbs. cubed chuck
2 T. shortening
1 lb. canned tomatoes
3 sliced onions
1/3 c. wine vinegar
1/2 c. molasses
8 carrots, 1" pieces
1/2 c. raisins
hot cooked rice

Combine first six ingredients, and sprinkle on meat, or toss in a plastic bag. Brown meat in shortening. Add next four ingredients and 1/2 cup water to meat in a stew pot. Simmer for approximately 2 hours, until meat is tender.

Add carrots and raisins. Simmer for 30 minutes, or until carrots are cooked. Serve with rice, cornbread, etc.

Vegetable Soup

Alanna Cunningham   *Italy*

Makes 4–6 servings
2–3 hours to cook

1/4 c. extra virgin olive oil
5 large white onions, chopped
5 cloves garlic, crushed and minced
2 leeks (white part only), chopped
4 large carrots, peeled and chopped
2 turnips, peeled and chopped
1 1/2 c. squash, peeled and chopped
6 new potatoes
10 leaves spinach
1 (16-oz.) can tomatoes, with juice
1/3 c. minced fresh parsley
1/4 c. minced fresh sage
1/4 c. minced fresh basil
salt and pepper to taste

Heat olive oil and add the next four ingredients. Sauté for seven minutes. Stir in remaining ingredients. Add water to cover and bring to a boil. Cover and simmer for 2-3 hours, stirring occasionally. Top off with parmesan cheese and serve.

Massachusetts Bay Scallop Bisque

Andrew Nawn's Mom   *United States*

Makes 4-6 servings

1 13 oz. can chicken broth
1 c. white wine
2 T. grated carrot
1 T. minced celery
1/2 c. minced onion
1 clove garlic, minced
1/2 t. curry
1/2 t. thyme
1 lb. bay scallops
1/4 c. butter
1/4 c. flour
1 c. milk

To make stock, combine first 8 ingredients and bring to a boil. Simmer for 15 minutes. Add scallops and poach for one minute. Strain stock and reserve solids and liquid.

In a large pot, melt 1/4 c. butter and stir in 1/4 c. flour, until smooth. Cook for 1/2 minute over low heat. Stir in strained stock and 1 cup milk. Bring to a boil and simmer for two minutes. Add scallops and solids.

Sue Weaver's 5-Hour Stew

Mom-Natalie

Makes 4-8 servings
5 hours to bake

1 1/2-2 lbs. stew meat
4-5 potatoes, peeled
6 carrots
1-2 onions, halved
celery
1 (2 lb.) can stewed tomatoes
1/2 c. cooking wine
3 T. minute tapioca
1 T. sugar
1 T. salt

Mix together the last five ingredients. Place this mixture along with the meat and vegetables in a heavy roaster and cover. Bake at 250° for 5 hours or longer.

Only a small percentage of all donations (12%) goes toward overhead and administration of the House, with the other 88% directly benefitting the families.

Salads &
Dressings

Robin's Caesar Salad

Robin Frank

Romaine lettuce
2 cloves garlic, crushed
5 T. olive oil
1 t. dijon mustard
2 T. grated Parmesan cheese
3 T. lemon juice
1 dash ground pepper
1 egg yolk
3/4 c. croutons
anchovy paste, to taste

Wash lettuce and tear into bite-size pieces. Wrap up and leave in a paper towel. Put all remaining ingredients in a bowl, adding anchovy paste one inch at a time. Wisk everything together. Put lettuce in a salad bowl, add the dressing, and mix well. Sprinkle parmesan cheese on top.

Research has shown that keeping families together during cancer therapy may increase the cure rate, and it does ease the pain and suffering caused by the disease and its treatment.

Hot Seafood Salad

Phyllis Light

25 minutes to bake

1/4 c. chopped celery
1/4 c. chopped onion
1/4 c. chopped green pepper
1/4 c. butter
1/2 lb. crabmeat, cooked or canned
1 lb. cooked shrimp, cut up
2 c. coarsely shredded or cubed Gouda or Edam cheese
1 c. mayonnaise
1/4 c. slivered almonds
1/4 c. lemon juice
1 T. lemon rind
1/2 t. salt
1/4 t. dry mustard
1/3 c. buttered bread crumbs

Sauté vegetables (celery, onion, and peppers) in 1/4 cup
butter. Combine remaining ingredients and mix with vegetables in a greased casserole pan. Sprinkle with 1/3 c. buttered
bread crumbs. Bake for 25 minutes at 325°.

Seven Layer Salad

Grandma Lil

1 head of lettuce
1/2 c. diced green peppers
1/2 c. diced celery
1/2 c. green onions, cut up
1/2 pkg. frozen green peas
1 c. mayonnaise
2 T. sugar
1 c. shredded cheddar cheese
8 slices crumbled bacon

Layer all of the ingredients in a deep bowl in the order
given. Cover and refrigerate overnight. Mix before serving.

Pepperoni, Mozzarella, and Broccoli Salad

Phyllis Light

45 minutes to prepare

1 lb. rigatoni
2/3 c. vegetable oil
1/4 c. lemon juice
2 T. red wine vinegar
1 t. salt
1 t. oregano
1/4 t. ground pepper
3 c. broccoli florets, steamed 3 minutes
1 12-oz. whole pepperoni, skinned and cut into 1/4" pieces
6 oz. mozzarella, cut into 1/4" pieces
1 medium green bell pepper, cut into 1/4" pieces
1/2 c. chopped red onion
1/2 c. chopped carrot
1/3 c. small black olives
1/4 c. chunked parmesan, about 1/4" size

Cook pasta in boiling salted water until al dente. Drain and rinse well with water. Whisk the oil, lemon juice, vinegar, salt, oregano, and black pepper together; set aside. In a large bowl, combine the cooked pasta, broccoli, pepperoni, mozzarella, bell pepper, red onion, carrot, olives and parmesan. Add dressing; toss to blend. Serve at room temperature.

Greek Marinade Salad

Susan and Steve   *Greece*

Makes 2-3 servings
Marinate chicken one day in advance, then 30 minutes to
    prepare salad next day

Marinade:
3/4 c. oil
1/2 c. lemon juice
1/4 c. fresh parsley, chopped
1 t. salt
1 t. oregano
1 t. thyme
1/2 t. ground pepper
4 chicken breasts, cut in strips or chunks

Salad:	Dressing:
Romaine lettuce	*2/3 c. olive oil*
3 green onions, chopped	*1/3 c. wine vinegar*
3 tomatoes	*1 t. salt*
1 lb. feta cheese, crumbled	*1 t. oregano*
1/4 lb. Kalamata olives	*ground pepper*

Prepare marinade by combining oil, lemon juice, parsley,
thyme, oregano, salt, and pepper. Marinate the chicken
overnight.

Prepare the salad in a bowl by combining the lettuce,
onions, tomatoes, cheese, and olives.

Make the salad dressing by combining the olive oil, vinegar, salt, oregano, and pepper. Shake well.

Fry or grill marinated chicken. Throw the chicken in the
salad while hot, pour the dressing on top, and serve.

Cheese Tortellini Salad

Carina and Andree Weidemand

Makes 4 servings
30 minutes to prepare

1/2 lb. tortellini
matchstick carrots
broccoli florets
1 bottle of Zesty Italian salad dressing
3–4 scallions, sliced
salt and pepper

Cook tortellini according to package directions. Blanch vegetables so that they are crisp and tender. Cool tortellini and vegetables. Toss tortellini, vegetables and Italian dressing together. Serve at room temperature or chilled. Season to taste.

Aunt Devota Wilson's Hot Chicken Salad

Lela Rotondo

Makes 8 servings
Prepare a day in advance

4 whole boneless chicken breasts (cut in half)
1 c. chopped celery
1 c. mayonnaise
1 c. chopped nuts
French dressing
1 can french fried onions

One day before serving, boil chicken, cool, and cut into bite-size pieces. Toss in the French dressing and marinate overnight.

The next day, add celery, nuts, and mayonnaise. Put salad in an oblong baking dish. Cook at 350° for 30 minutes. Add the can of onions and cook for another 5 minutes.

Tortellini Rosa Salad
(hot or cold)

Denise Bomberger   *Italy*

Serves 4 as an entree; 6 as a side dish
40 minutes to prepare

1 lb. cheese tortellini
4 large diced plum tomatoes
1/2 medium diced red onion
handful of chopped parsley
1/4 c. romano or parmesan cheese
1 c. mayonnaise
1/4 c. red wine vinegar
dash of nutmeg

Cook tortellini in salted water. Rinse with cold water if serving cold. Drain tortellini. Add tomatoes, onion, parsley, and
romano cheese. Gently stir.

Combine mayonnaise, vinegar, and nutmeg. Pour as
much as desired over tortellini.

Bacon, Shrimp, and Avocado Salad

Virginia Brown   *United States*

Makes 4 servings

1 (16-oz.) pkg. frozen, shelled and deveined shrimp
2 T. dry sherry
1/4 lbs. sliced bacon
1/2 c. mayonnaise
2 T. cider vinegar
2 T. water
1 T. lemon juice
1/2 t. sugar
1/8 t. ground red pepper
1 (10-oz.) bag spinach
2 medium-size avocados
1 (4-oz.) jar pimentos, drained and diced

Place shrimp with a little bit of water in a 9-inch pie plate.
Cook on high in a microwave for 9 to 10 minutes, stirring
occasionally. Drain, sprinkle with sherry, cover, and refrigerate shrimp while preparing the rest of the salad.

Place bacon on double thickness of paper towels on
paper plate. Cook on high, in the microwave, for 5 to 6 minutes, until browned. Crumble the bacon strips.

In a small bowl, beat mayonnaise, water, vinegar, lemon
juice, sugar and red pepper together. Set aside.

Line a large platter with spinach. Cut each avocado in
half, discard seed, peel, cut into thin slices, and arrange on
spinach. With slotted spoon, place shrimp on spinach, and
sprinkle with pimento and bacon. Serve with dressing on
the side.

Tuna Pasta Salad

Eileen Moore

Makes 4 servings
Approximately 20 minutes to prepare

1 can tuna
1 pkg. frozen peas
1 pkg. frozen corn
1/2 pkg. of pasta shells
2 t. mayonnaise
salt and pepper

Boil pasta until desired tenderness. Cook peas and corn. Mix together tuna and mayonnaise. Add cooked pasta, peas, and corn. Chill and serve.

French Salad

Ruth Lynch   *France*

Makes 4 servings

1 head escarole
1/4 lb. fresh spinach
1 can mandarin oranges
1/2 red onion, thinly sliced
1/4 lb. bleu cheese, crumbled

Combine ingredients and toss with favorite French dressing.

Grilled Bangkok Beef Salad

Pat Baird   *Thailand*

12 oz. lean top round (for London Broil)
1/4 c. fresh lime juice
1 T. and 1 t. rice vinegar
2 t. fish sauce (nam pla*) or low sodium soy sauce
1/4 t. crushed red pepper flakes, or to taste
3 c. torn spinach
3 c. torn romaine lettuce leaves
1 medium tomato, cored and cut into 6 wedges
1/2 c. shredded carrot
1/2 c. bean sprouts
1/2 c. thinly sliced red onion
1/4 c. chopped fresh mint leaves, for garnish

Preheat grill or broiler. Cook steak about 5 minutes on each side or until done as desired. Set aside or wrap in aluminum foil and refrigerate until ready to use. Then slice across the grain into very thin slices.

In a large bowl, combine lime juice, rice vinegar, fish or soy sauce, and pepper. Add steak and remaining ingredients except the red onion and mint. Toss well.

Transfer the salad to a large platter and garnish with red onion and mint.

* Available at Asian markets

Bleu Cheese Dressing

Andrew Nawn's Mom   *France*

Prepare one day in advance; 15 minutes to prepare

3/4 c. sour cream
1/2 t. dry mustard
1/2 t. black pepper
1/2 t. salt
1/3 t. garlic powder
1 t. Worcestershire sauce
1/3 c. mayonnaise
4 oz. bleu cheese

Blend first 6 ingredients together for 2 minutes at low speed.
Add mayonnaise and blend for 2 minutes at medium speed.
Crumble in bleu cheese, blend for 4 minutes. Let sit for 24
hours before serving.

Main Dishes

Grilled Pineapple Ginger Swordfish

Susan Birnbaum

20 minutes to prepare

10 oz. swordfish steak
1/4 c. unsweetened pineapple juice
1/4 c. dry white wine
1 1/2 t. coarsely grated ginger
1 clove garlic, minced

Preheat broiler. Wash and dry fish. Combine pineapple juice, wine, ginger, and garlic in a small bowl. Add swordfish and marinate for about 10 minutes. Broil swordfish for 8 to 10 minutes, basting occasionally.

Salmon or tuna patties

Grandma Lil

1 can salmon or tuna
1/2 c. sour cream
1/2 c. corn flakes
2 eggs
1 T. minced onion
2 onions

Mix together all ingredients, except onions. Form into patties and fry in oil. Brown 2 onions, until golden, and put on top of patties when served.

Salmon mousse

Eileen Hochheiser

5 minutes to prepare; set overnight

1 envelope Knox gelatin
1/2 c. water
2 T. lemon juice
1 medium onion
1 heaping t. dillweed
1 c. mayonnaise
1 c. red salmon
1/2 t. paprika
1/2 c. sour cream

Soften gelatin in lemon juice. Dissolve in boiling water. Run in a blender for 30 seconds. Add onion; run in blender for another 30 seconds. Add salmon, mayonnaise, paprika, and sour cream. Run blender for another 30 seconds.

Place in greased mold. Chill for several hours or overnight.

Mexican Baked Fish

Judy King   *Mexico*

Serves 4
30 minutes to prepare

4 fish fillets (St. Peter's Fish, Snapper, Sea Bass)
Nonstick spray coating
1/4 c. bread crumbs
dash garlic powder
salt and pepper to taste
3/4 c. salsa
1 T. cilantro, chopped.

Spray oven-proof dish with nonstick spray. Place fish in dish and sprinkle with bread crumbs and seasonings. Bake at 500° for 12-15 minutes. Top fish with salsa. Sprinkle with cilantro. A low-fat, low-cholesterol dish that goes well with rice or baked potato.

More than 110 weekly volunteers and numerous corporate groups give their time to the House.

Gravlax

Denise Rochon and Bob Franck

2 lbs. fresh salmon (center cuts)
1/4 c. salt
3/4 c. sugar
Plenty of fresh dill, chopped
2 t. white pepper

Sauce:
3 T. oil
1 T. red wine vinegar
1 T. sugar
1/3 t. salt
3 T. prepared mustard
3 T. dill

Mix salt and sugar. Rub this mixture into the fish. Sprinkle some in enamelware with some dill and lay salmon in bottom of pan. Sprinkle generously with dill (thick layer), sugar and salt mixture, and pepper. Put more salmon on top. Sprinkle with remaining salt and sugar mixture.

Wrap fish in lightweight aluminum foil. "Leach" for 4-5 hours with heavy plate, pour off liquid. Refrigerate at least 48 hours, turning fish twice. Combine remaining ingredients to make a sauce for this dish. Stores 1-2 weeks.

Parmesan Baked Fish

Judy King   *United States*

Makes 4 servings
30 minutes to prepare

4 fish fillets (cod, salmon, orange roughy)
nonstick spray coating
1/3 c. mayonnaise
2 T. grated parmesan cheese
2 T. snipped fresh chives or sliced green onions
1/2 t. white wine Worcestshire sauce

In a small bowl, stir together mayonnaise, parmesan cheese, chives or green onion, and Worcestshire sauce. Place fish fillets in baking dish coated with nonstick spray. Spread mayonnaise mixture over fish fillets. Bake uncovered at 450° for 12 to 15 minutes or until fish flakes easily when tested with fork.

More than 75% of the children who stay at the Ronald McDonald House are undergoing treatment not yet available anywhere else in the world.

Shrimp Creole

Rona Gabin   *United States*

Makes 4 servings

1/4 c. green pepper strips
1/4 c. onions
1 clove garlic, minced
1 T. butter
1 t. lemon juice
1 can tomato soup
1/3 c. water
dash soy sauce
1 lb. small cooked shrimp
2 c. cooked rice

In saucepan, cook pepper, onions, and garlic in butter until tender. Add remaining ingredients except rice. Heat, stirring every now and then. Serve over rice. For extra spice, add Tabasco sauce while cooking.

Shrimp Marinade Bake

Marguerite Basti

1 1/2 hours to prepare

1 1/2 lbs. shrimp
1/2 c. olive oil
2 T. lemon juice
1 T. mild barbecue sauce
2 T. chopped parsley
1 T. soy sauce
2 T. duck sauce

Mix all ingredients, except shrimp, and toss. Add shrimp and refrigerate for 1 hour. Bake at 450° for 10 minutes. Serve with French bread and lemon wedges.

Uncle Mike's Grilled Swordfish

1lb. = 2-3 servings
30 minutes to prepare

swordfish, 1 1/2-2" thick
real lemon juice
medium to dry white wine
olive oil
Adobo seasoning
hickory or mesquite woodchips

Marinate swordfish overnight, or for at least 4-6 hours, in lemon juice, wine, and olive oil. Use 3 to 1 lemon juice to wine and oil to taste. Add adobo seasoning to both sides when you turn the fish midway through the marinating cycle. Save marinade sauce.

Soak woodchips in water for at least one hour, the longer the better. Drain water and put woodchips on a pie plate and place on hot coals inside grill. Grill the swordfish with the grill cover closed so that the woodchip smoke is effective. Swordfish should be brown on both sides. Baste and add additional adobo seasoning with each turn.

When it is done cooking, place the fish again in the leftover marinade, and put the fish back on the grill (low flame) for a few extra minutes with the cover closed to complete the flavor (5 minutes maximum).

Serve the fish with medium to dry white wine and a few lemon slices. The fish is cooked when it feels firm.

Stir-Fried Shrimp

Betty Lou Smith   *China*

Makes 4 servings

1 lb. medium size shrimp, shelled and de-veined
1 egg white
2 t. corn starch
1/2 t. salt
2 c. peanut or corn oil
2 t. minced fresh ginger or 1/2 t. ground ginger
1 clove garlic, minced
1/4 - 1/2 t. crushed red pepper

Sherry sauce:
1 t. sugar
1 t. cornstarch
2 T. soy sauce
1 T. dry sherry
1 T. water
1 t. vinegar

Split shrimp in half lengthwise, rinse, and dry on paper towel. Combine egg whites, corn starch and salt in a medium-sized bowl. Add shrimp and toss until coated. Refrigerate 1 to 24 hours.

Heat oil in wok or deep skillet to 300°. Add shrimp, stir-fry 1-2 minutes, or until shrimp changes color. Separate, as you pour shrimp and oil into strainer over a bowl.

Prepare sherry sauce by mixing all sauce ingredients well. Re-heat wok, return 2 T. drained oil to wok. Add ginger, stir-fry 5 seconds. Add garlic and pepper, stir-fry for 5 seconds. Add shrimp and stir-fry 1 minute. Stir sherry sauce to combine. Pour in sherry sauce, stirring until thickened and coating the shrimp.

Serve with rice.

Dill Salmon

Eileen Moore

Makes 1 serving
20 minutes to bake

1 salmon steak   *fresh dill*
1 t. mayonnaise   *salt and pepper*
3 t. white wine

Combine salmon steak with mayonnaise, fresh dill, white wine, salt, and pepper. Cover with foil and place in oven for 20 minutes at 350°.

Honest-to-Goodness Crab Cakes

B. Bush   *Maryland*

Makes 4 servings

1 large egg
3 T. mayonnaise
2 T. chopped, fresh parsley
1 T. fresh lemon juice
1 t. Dijon mustard
1/2 t. salt
1/4 t. ground red pepper
1 lb. lump crabmeat, flaked and picked over
1/2 c. fresh bread crumbs
1/3 c. plain dry bread crumbs
2 T. butter or margarine

Whisk first seven ingredients in a large bowl. Add crabmeat and fresh bread crumbs. Mix well.

Line cookie sheet with wax paper. Using 1/3 cup measure, shape crab mixture into eight 1" thick patties. Coat lightly with dry bread crumbs. Refrigerate 1 to 8 hours.

Melt butter in a large non-stick skillet over medium/high heat. Add crab cakes and cook until golden, 3 minutes per side. Serve with tartar sauce if desired.

Psari Savori (fish fillets in wine sauce)

Greece

Makes 5 servings

2 lbs. porgy fillets or substitute other lean white fish fillets
1 t. salt
1/2 c. flour
1 c. cooking oil
1 1/2 c. canned, peeled tomatoes
1 t. tomato paste
3 T. red wine vinegar
1/2 t. finely chopped garlic
1 large bay leaf, crumbled
1 t. salt
1/4 t. black pepper

Wash and pat dry the fish fillets. Sprinkle with salt and coat with flour.

In a large skillet, cook fillets in hot oil for 3 minutes over a medium flame. Drain fillets of excess oil. With remaining oil in skillet, add peeled tomatoes, tomato paste, vinegar, garlic, bay leaf, salt, and pepper.

Bring to a boil, stirring many times. Cook until most of the juices are absorbed. Pour the sauce over the fillets and cool before serving.

Salmon

United States

Makes 4 servings
20 minutes to cook

A little melted butter
2 onions, sliced
sprigs of fresh dill, parsley, or thyme
4 salmon steaks
salt and freshly ground black pepper
1 lemon
1 1/2 oz. butter
6 oz. virtually fat-free fromage frais
75 g. pack of fresh watercress, chopped

Brush 4 sheets of foil with melted butter. Divide the onion between each piece of foil, and place a sprig of dill on the onion. Place one salmon steak on top of the dill and onion, and squeeze lemon juice over salmon. Add seasoning to taste and a dab of butter.

Wrap the foil around the fish to form a parcel and place on a baking tray in a preheated oven at 350°. Cook for 20 minutes.

Meanwhile, pour the fromage frais into a bowl and stir in chopped watercress with seasoning to taste. Remove the salmon from the foil and serve with the sauce.

Scrod in Olive and Horseradish sauce

Rosalind Axelrod   *France*

Makes 4 servings
Approximately 45 minutes to prepare

4 scrod fillets, about 1 1/2 inches thick (5 to 6 oz. each)
1/2 c. chopped onion
1 c. dry, fruity white wine
1/2 t. salt
1/2 t. freshly ground black pepper
about 12 oil-cured black olives
2 T. small capers
2 T. horseradish
1/4 c. sour cream
4 T. coarsely chopped cilantro

Place scrod, onion, wine, salt, and pepper in a stainless steel saucepan. Bring to a boil over high heat. Cover, reduce heat to low, and boil gently for two minutes (the scrod will be undercooked at this point).

With a slotted spoon, carefully transfer scrod to a platter, cover it, and set aside so that it continues to cook in its own residual heat.

Meanwhile, add the olives, capers, horseradish, and sour cream to the saucepan and bring to a boil. Arrange the scrod fillets on separate plates, and top with the sauce. Sprinkle with the cilantro and serve immediately.

Jeanne's Birthday Chicken

Jen Breuer   *United States*

1/2 c. chicken broth   2 bay leaves
1/2 c. dry white wine   2 T. oregano
1 oz. dried cèpes or morels   1 T. basil
   (or fresh mushrooms)   pepper
1/4 c. olive oil
2 chickens (2 1/2 - 3 lbs. each),
   cut into 8 pieces each
12 cloves garlic
2 c. diced onions
1/4 c. brandy
6 c. chopped, drained, canned or fresh, plum tomatoes
1/2 c. pitted Kalamatu or Niçoise olives
1/4 c. coarsely chopped sun-dried tomatoes
4 oz. anchovy fillets, drained and coarsely chopped
3 T. capers, drained
1 T. red wine vinegar
1/2 c. chopped Italian parsley

Combine stock, wine and dried mushrooms in a small
saucepan. Bring to a boil, reduce heat, and simmer for 15
minutes. Set the mixture aside.

Heat oil in covered saucepan. Add chicken in small
batches and sauté on both sides. Transfer to platter.

Mince 8 cloves of garlic, add to saucepan with onions.
Cook about 5 minutes, until tender. Return chicken to pan.
Add brandy and carefully flame, shaking pan until flame
subsides.

Add plum tomatoes, olives, sun-dried tomatoes,
anchovies, capers, vinegar, bay leaves, oregano, basil, pepper and mushroom mixture with liquid to chicken. Stir well,
cover and simmer for 30 minutes. Transfer chicken to serving platter. Mince remaining garlic and all but 1 T. of
parsley. Add to chicken sauce and simmer, uncovered, for 5
minutes. Spoon sauce over chicken, sprinkle with remaining
parsley and serve.

Pollo Alla Casciatoro
(Chicken Hunter's Style)

Phyllis Vaccaro   *Italy*

Makes 4-5 servings
1 1/2 hours to prepare

1 frying chicken, 4 lbs.
4 small onions, chopped
5 T. olive oil
1/2 c. flour
salt and pepper to taste
1 clove garlic, chopped
1 c. canned tomatoes
1 c. sliced mushrooms
1 large green pepper

Cut chicken into serving pieces. Season with salt and pepper, and roll lightly in the flour. Heat oil in a skillet, and brown chicken on all sides for about 10 minutes. Stem, seed, and slice green pepper lengthwise. Mix with onions, garlic, and tomatoes. Add mixture to chicken in skillet.

Cover and simmer slowly for 40 minutes. Add mushrooms and simmer for another 15 minutes or until chicken and mushrooms are tender. Serve very hot.

Chicken Breast with Garlic and Balsamic Vinegar

Gail Mautner

Makes 4 servings
45-60 minutes to prepare

4 boneless, skinless chicken breasts, halved (about 1 1/4 lbs.)
salt and freshly ground pepper to taste
3/4 lb. small to medium-sized mushrooms
2 T. flour
2 T. olive oil
6 cloves garlic, peeled
1/4 c. balsamic vinegar
3/4 c. fresh or canned chicken broth
1 bay leaf
1/2 t. minced, fresh thyme or 1/4 t. dried thyme
1 T. butter

Separate chicken fillets and season with salt and pepper.

Rinse mushrooms, drain, and pat dry.

Season flour with salt and pepper. Dredge chicken through the mixture and shake off any excess. Heat oil in a heavy skillet over medium-high heat. Cook chicken until browned on one side (about 3 minutes). Add garlic cloves.

Turn chicken pieces and scatter mushrooms over them. Cook for another 3 minutes, and then add vinegar, broth, bay leaf, and thyme. Cover tightly and cook over medium-low heat for 10 minutes, turning pieces occasionally.

Transfer chicken to a warm serving platter and cover with foil. Cook sauce with mushrooms, uncovered, over medium-high heat for 7 minutes. Swirl in butter.

Discard bay leaf, and pour mushrooms and sauce over chicken and serve.

Chicken or Veal Marsala

Carol Brandes

30 minutes to bake

8 whole boneless breasts or 3 lbs. veal cutlets pounded to 1/8"
  thickness
5 T. corn oil
1/2 lb. fresh sliced mushrooms
1 t. minced garlic
1 t. onion powder
1/2 t. marjarom
4 cubes chicken bouillon, dissolved in 2 c. boiling water
1 c. Marsala wine
1/2 t. salt
1/2 t. pepper
1 t. flour
1 t. tomato paste

Preheat oven to 350°. Coat chicken in a mixture of flour, salt, and pepper. Brown lightly in 3 T. corn oil in a pan. Remove and place in a 13" x 9" baking dish. In a pan, sauté mushrooms and onion powder in 2 T. oil. Add garlic, tomato paste, marjoram, 1/2 t. salt, 1/8 t. pepper, 1 t. flour, chicken stock, and wine. Simmer for 5 minutes after mixture comes to boil. Pour mixture over chicken and cover with foil. Bake for 30 minutes at 350°.

Lemon Chicken

Barbara Grace   *Japan*

Makes 4 servings

1/4 c. sesame seeds
1/2 c. seasoned dry bread crumbs
1 egg beaten
4 boneless chicken breasts
vegetable oil

Sauce:
1/3 c. lemon juice
2 t. soy sauce
2-3 T. sugar
1 T. corn starch
1 c. water

Combine sesame seeds and bread crumbs. Dip chicken into egg, then roll in crumbs. Set aside for 10 minutes, then fry in vegetable oil until golden. Set chicken aside.

In a pan, combine lemon juice, soy sauce, sugar, and water; add corn starch and bring to a boil. Stir until thick. Spoon over chicken.

Baked Chicken and Rice

Grandma Lil

Makes 4 servings
1 hour to bake

4 chicken cutlets
1 c. uncooked white rice
1 pkg. onion soup mix
3 c. water

In a bowl, mix together rice, onion soup mix, and water.
Pour mixture in a greased pan over the chicken and bake at
350° for 30 minutes. Uncover and bake another 30 minutes
(until rice is done) and casserole is slightly brown on top.

*With the completion of its new House in December 1992, the
Ronald McDonald House of NYC achieved its goal of provid-
ing the largest home of its kind in the world.*

Chicken and Broccoli

Grandma Lil

Bakes 15 minutes

1 bunch fresh broccoli, cooked and drained
1 1/2 c. cooked chicken, cut into pieces
1/3 c. milk
1 can Campbell's Cream of Broccoli soup
1/2 c. shredded cheddar cheese
1 T. melted butter
2 T. bread crumbs

In a 9" pie plate or casserole, lay broccoli and top with chicken. Combine soup and milk and pour over chicken. Sprinkle with cheese. Combine butter and bread crumbs, sprinkle over cheese. Bake at 450° about 15 minutes.

Debbie D's Delicious Chicken

Debbie Danuff   *United States*

Makes 6 servings
1 1/2 hours to prepare

1 bottle French dressing
1 box minute rice
3/4 c. chopped onions
6 pieces chicken
paprika

Boil the chicken pieces in water for approximately 15 minutes. Take out of water and scrape the skin with the back of a knife while running under cold water. Put dressing and onions in a saucepan and bring to a boil. After sauce boils, cover and lower heat.

Place chicken in sauce and mix to cover all of the chicken. Leave in sauce with cover on for 30 minutes. Take chicken out of saucepan and place in a baking pan. Sprinkle paprika on top and bake in a 350° oven for 15 minutes. Serve with minute rice.

Stuffed Chicken

Joanna Piccione

1 pkg. boneless chicken
1 1/2 c. plain bread crumbs
1/2 T. garlic, pepper, parsley, oregano
1/2 c. white wine
2-3 T. olive oil
1/2 c. spinach (chopped, cooked, and drained)
1/2 c. mushrooms, diced
1/2 c. parmesan cheese

Combine all ingredients except chicken, wine, and olive oil to make stuffing. Then add wine and olive oil to mixture until the bread crumbs are moist. Take 1 T. of stuffing and roll in middle of chicken. Put extra bread crumbs on outside of chicken. Bake about 20 minutes at 350°.

Honey Mustard Baked Chicken Breast

Joan Taub

Makes 8 servings
40 minutes to bake

8 pieces chicken breasts
salt and pepper to taste
1/2 c. honey
4 T. melted sweet butter
1/4 c. Dijon mustard

Preheat oven to 350°. Season breasts with salt and pepper.
Combine butter, honey, and mustard. Spoon half of sauce
into 2 shallow baking dishes. Add breasts and turn to coat
well. Turn and baste once with remaining sauce after 15
minutes. Bake uncovered for 30-40 minutes or until cooked
through.

Sesame Glazed Chicken

Debbie Spey

Makes 2-4 servings
1 hour to prepare

2 whole boneless breasts of chicken (4 single breasts)
1 T. cornstarch
1/4 c. chicken broth
2 T. vegetable (olive) oil
2 T. soy sauce
1 t. sesame oil
2 T. mirin (Japanese rice wine)
1 t. sugar
sesame seeds, toasted (optional)

Cut chicken into 1-2 inch chunks; dry, and sprinkle with cornstarch.

In a large sauté pan, heat vegetable and sesame oil. Sauté chicken until white.

Mix together broth, soy sauce, mirin, sugar. Add sauce to chicken. Simmer for 5 minutes until sauce reduces by two-thirds. Increase heat for 10-30 seconds to glaze chicken.

Serve over rice. Sprinkle with sesame seeds, if desired. Serve with a green vegetable, snow peas, broccoli, sugar snap peas, or green peas.

Turkey Breast With Fruit Dressing

Fran Sharp

1 c. chopped celery
1/4 c. chopped onion
4 oz. butter or margarine
4 medium apples, diced
1/2 c. seedless raisins
1/2 c. seedless prunes
1 t. poultry seasoning
1 t. allspice
2 c. bread stuffing
1/2 c. apple juice
3-4 lbs. boneless turkey breast

Soak raisins and prunes in warm water, then drain. Sauté celery and onion in butter or margarine. Add seasonings. Then add apples, raisins, prunes, and stuffing. Mix well. Moisten if necessary with apple juice.

Place mixture in a shallow pan. Cover with turkey breast pieces, or one large deboned piece. Roast at 350° until breast is done (approximately 15-20 minutes per pound). Baste with butter and apple juice.

This can also be made in a crock pot and left to cook on low for 3-4 hours.

Chicken Divan

Linda Huss

Baking time approximately 45 minutes

1 boned chicken
1 can cream of mushroom soup
1/2 c. mayonnaise
1/4 c. lemon juice
1 t. curry
1 head broccoli

Boil chicken (save the broth) and break into small pieces. Steam broccoli and cut into bite-size pieces. Layer chicken and broccoli in casserole.

Mix soup, mayonnaise, curry, broth, and lemon thoroughly and pour over casserole. Bake at 350° for half an hour covered, and 15 minutes uncovered. Be careful not to overcook.

Chicken Picata

Ethel Dosso *Italy*

Makes 2 servings

1 lb. skinned and deboned chicken breasts, cut into
bite-size pieces
4 oz. butter
1 oz. oil
juice of 1 lemon
1 T. lemon peel
1 can artichokes, drained and cut into quarters
paprika

Sauté chicken in butter and oil, stirring frequently for five
minutes. Add the juice of half of the lemon, lemon peel, and
artichoke. Simmer for an additional three minutes and place
on a warm serving platter. Squeeze the other half of the
lemon over the top, and sprinkle with paprika.

Crescent Chicken Sandwiches

Virginia

Makes 4 servings

2 T. margarine
3 oz. cream cheese
2 c. cooked, cubed chicken
1 T. chopped onion
1/4 t. salt
1/8 t. pepper
1-2 T. milk
tube of crescent rolls
bread crumbs

Mix margarine and cream cheese together. Mix next five ingredients together and combine with margarine mixture. Place rolls into 4 squares, and divide chicken mixture into the 4 squares. Pull covers of rolls up, press together, and seal seams. Brush with butter and sprinkle with bread crumbs. Bake at 375° for 20-25 minutes.

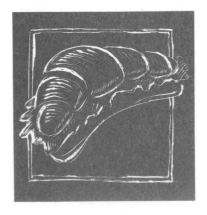

Chicken Marbella

24 hours to prepare, 1 hour to bake

4 chickens cut in fourths or eighths
1 clove garlic (peeled and pureed)
1/4 c. oregano
salt & pepper to taste
1/2 c. red wine vinegar
1/2 c. olive oil
1 c. pitted prunes
1/2 c. spanish olives
1/2 c. capers with juice
6 bay leaves
1 c. brown sugar
1 c. white wine

In a large bowl combine chicken, garlic, oregano, pepper, salt, vinegar, oil, prunes, olives, capers, and bay leaves. Cover and let marinate in refrigerator overnight.

The next day, preheat oven to 350°. Place chicken in single layer in 1 or 2 baking dishes. Spoon marinade over chicken evenly. Sprinkle brown sugar over chicken and pour white wine around chicken.

Bake approximately 60 minutes, basting frequently with pan juices.

Chilled Chicken Rolls Morengo-Style

Susan Dent

25 minutes to bake

1/4 c. unseasoned bread crumbs
1 T. parmesan cheese
2 large chicken breasts
2 slices thin ham
2 slices thin Monterey Jack
1/2 medium tomato, chopped
1 t. fresh basil, chopped
1 t. chopped parsley
1 1/2 T. melted butter

Lightly grease an 8" x 8" x 2" square pan. Combine crumbs, parmesan, and dash of pepper on wax paper. Set aside.

Pound chicken breasts, smooth side down, between wax paper to 1/4 inch thick. Place ham and cheese on breast, folding to 1/2 inch smaller than flattened breasts.

Sprinkle tomato, basil, parsley and a dash of pepper over each breast. Roll up egg-roll style, tucking ends in as you roll.

Brush each roll all over with melted butter. Roll in crumb mixture to coat completely. Place in prepared pan, seam side down. Let stand 15 minutes to set crumbs.

Bake rolls in pre-heated 375° oven for 25 minutes until golden and slightly firm to touch. Let cool in refrigerator. Cover and chill several hours or overnight.

To serve, cut rolls 1/4 inch thick and arrange on a bed of wild rice salad.

American Rock Cornish Game Hens with Cranberry-Orange Glaze

Barbara L. Bush   *United States*

Makes 4 servings
1 to 1 1/4 hours to cook

4 cornish game hens
1/2 c. butter, melted
1/2 c. whole berry cranberry sauce
1/2 c. orange marmalade
1/2 c. mandarin orange segments
3 T. lemon juice
1 T. minced onion

Rinse hens and pat dry. Coat inside and out with butter. Place hens on rack in shallow roasting pan. Roast in pre-heated oven at 425° for 15 minutes. Reduce heat to 375° and roast for an additional 45 minutes to 1 hour, basting occasionally with drippings.

Combine remaining ingredients to make a glaze. Brush hens with glaze during last 20 minutes of roasting. Glaze again before serving.

Hungarian Goulash

Mari Pinter   *Hungary*

Makes 4-6 servings
1 hour to prepare

1 lb. beef round roast
1 lb. beef chuck
3 T. vegetable oil
1/2 c. finely chopped onion
1 T. paprika
1 t. salt
1 t. caraway seeds
2 T. tomato paste
1 c. beef broth
4 medium potatoes
8 c. water
1 medium green pepper, seeded and cut into strips

Cut meat into 1" cubes. In a medium dutch oven pot, heat oil over medium heat for 1 minute. Add onions and sauté.

Add paprika, beef cubes, salt, caraway seeds and cook for 10 minutes, stirring often.

In a small bowl, stir tomato paste into 1/2 c. beef broth. Add to beef mixture and stir. Simmer for 30 minutes.

Peel potatoes and cut into bite-size pieces. Add potatoes, rest of beef broth, and 8 cups of water to pot. Begin to boil and then simmer for 15 minutes.

Return soup to a boil, add pepper strips, and cook for 10 more minutes.

Although many people think that goulash is a thick stew, this Hungarian goulash is a substantial soup. It is usually served as a main dish followed by a non-meat second dish or dessert.

Orange Brisket

Aunt Sylvia

1 1/2 hours to cook

1 brisket of beef, first cut
carrots
1 large onion, diced
1/4 c. ketchup
1 pkg. George Washington Golden Powder
1 large glass water
paprika

Put diced onions in the bottom of a roasting pan. Slice lots of carrots and put in pan. Mix ketchup, water and powder; put in bottom of pan.

Place meat in pan and cover with paprika. Cover pan and cook for 1 1/2 hours at 350°. Turn after 1 hour and cook until tender (30 more minutes). Cook with cover off for the last 30 minutes; add more paprika.

Brisket

Carolyn Belinsky   *European/Jewish*

Takes 2 days to make

4 lbs. brisket
3 large onions, sauteed
cloves of garlic, to taste
salt and pepper to taste
24 oz. ketchup
18 oz. water
1 c. brown sugar
6 dried apricot strips, broken up

Prepare sauce by mixing ketchup, water, sugar, and apricot together. Pour sauce over meat. Put all ingredients in a deep tin pan and cover with tin foil. Cook for 2 hours.

Slice when cool and put meat back in sauce. Cook for 2 hours the next day and serve.

Borekas (meat pastry)

Anne Fuchs   *Turkey*

Makes 8 servings
15 minutes to mix; 40 minutes to bake

1 pkg. of 8 frozen pastry squares
1 small pkg. of chopped meat (turkey, veal, or beef)
1 pkg. of onion soup mix
1 egg
1/2 c. corn flake crumbs
2 T. chopped cilantro
1/2 - 1 c. water

Defrost pastry squares and place on greased cookie sheet.

In a medium sized bowl, mix all other ingredients together. Add water as needed to make mixture soft, but not liquid.

Place a generous tablespoon of the mixture in the center of the pastry squares and fold with a fork into a triangle.

Bake at 350° for 40 minutes or until the pastry is golden brown. Note: Extra meat can be cooked in a broth or marinara sauce and served as a meat sauce on top of the pastry.

Shepherd's Pie

Eileen Moore   *Ireland*

Makes 6 servings
40 minutes to bake

1 lb. ground beef
1 t. cooking oil
2 onions, chopped
1 packet oxtail soup
2 lbs. potatoes
1 lb. carrots
1 pkg. frozen peas
salt and pepper to taste

Heat oil in pan, add meat and onions, and cook until browned.

Peel and boil potatoes and carrots together. Mash when cooked. Cook peas according to package. Mix soup with 3/4 pint water. Mix together meat, onions, peas, soup, salt and pepper. Place in a foil tray and place potatoes and carrots on top. Bake in oven at 350° for 40 minutes.

The cost to support one family for one night is $140, but the family is charged only $20—about 10% of the cost of an average New York City hotel room—and we waive the fee if the family cannot afford it.

Sausage and Peppers

Marianne Huss   *Italy*

Makes 4-6 servings
45 minutes to prepare

8 spicy Italian sausages, parboiled 5 mins.
2 large onions, sliced
3 green peppers, strip cut
2 tomatoes, cut in chunks
1 T. oregano
1 clove fresh garlic, minced
salt and pepper
olive oil

Sauté onions and garlic in a small amount of olive oil. Add parboiled sausages, cut into chunks, and brown over low flame. When onions and sausages are golden, add all remaining ingredients and simmer over low heat for 30 minutes. Serve with boiled new potatoes and garlic bread.

Sweet and Sour Meatballs

Carolyn Belinsky   *United States*

2 lbs. chopped meat, lean
2 eggs
onion flakes, enough for flavor
3/4 c. bread crumbs
garlic to taste
salt and pepper to taste
large onion, cut up in bottom of large sauce pot
handful of white raisins
1 large can tomato sauce
1/2 c. sugar
1 lemon, squeezed

Mix chopped meat, eggs, onion flakes, bread crumbs, garlic, salt and pepper in a bowl. Form into meat balls.

Put meat balls on top of onions, and cover with water. Add handful of white raisins and salt. Bring to a boil. Clean off top layer and simmer for 15 minutes. Serve over rice if desired.

To make sweet and sour sauce, pour tomato sauce, sugar, and lemon juice into a pot and cook for 30 minutes. Add salt to taste.

Simple Goulash

Linda Huss   *Hungary*

Makes 4 servings

3/4 lb. ground beef
4 strips bacon (may use cooking oil instead)
1 medium onion, chopped
3-4 potatoes, peeled and cubed
1 (2 lb.) can tomatoes
salt and pepper to taste

On top of stove in a 2-quart saucepan, fry the bacon. When crisp, crumble and leave in pan while browning ground beef and onions.

After cooking well, add tomatoes, and season to taste with salt and pepper. Simmer for 10-15 minutes. Add cubed potatoes. Continue cooking gently until potatoes are tender.

Tastes great an hour or two later.

Enchilada Pie

Amy Resnikoff   *Mexico*

Makes 4 servings
Bakes for 30 minutes

1 can tomato paste
1 (2 lb.) can black olives, pitted and sliced
1 lb. Monterey Jack cheese, grated
1 lb. ground beef
1 onion, sliced
salt, pepper, garlic powder, chili powder to taste
6 tortillas

Brown beef and onions with spices. Add tomato paste and
1 1/2 c. water. Cook until water absorbs.

In a casserole dish, layer tortilla, meat mix, cheese, and
olives. Repeat until dish is full. Bake at 375° for 30 minutes.

*More than 3,500 children and their families have stayed in
the Ronald McDonald House of NYC over the last 10 years.*

Aunt Sylvia's Meatballs

Aunt Sylvia

1 to 1 1/2 hours to cook

Meatballs:
2 lbs. ground beef or turkey
bread crumbs
egg
garlic powder
minced onions
parsley

Sauce:
1 (15 oz.) can tomato sauce
1 pkg. George Washington powder
1 large onion
pepper
Worcestershire sauce

Sauté diced onion in pan. Add tomato sauce and the same amount of water. Add pepper, powder, and dash of Worcestshire sauce. Bring to a boil; lower heat and simmer. For meatballs, mix meat, bread crumbs, seasoning and egg together; shape into small balls. Add meatballs to sauce and simmer for 1 to 1 1/2 hours.

Jamaican Pork

Judy King   *Jamaica*

Makes 4 servings

2 T. butter
1 t. curry powder
2 medium bananas
1 lb. pork tenderloin, cubed
1/2 c. pineapple juice
1/2 c. onion, minced
1 clove garlic, minced
1/4 c. flaked coconut

Melt butter in large skillet. Stir in curry powder. Cut bananas into 1/2 inch round pieces and sauté in curry butter until golden. Remove bananas from skillet and set aside.

Add pork cubes to skillet and sauté until golden brown. Add salt to taste. Stir in pineapple juice, garlic, and onion. Cover and simmer for 10 minutes until pork cubes are tender. Stir in coconut and bananas and toss lightly. Serve with hot cooked rice.

Meatloaf

Denise Bomberger   *United States*

Makes 2-4 servings
1 hour to cook

1 lb. ground beef
2/3 c. oatmeal
salt
1/2 c. grated cheddar cheese
1/4 c. diced onion
1 egg
2/3 c. milk
1/3 c. ketchup
1 T. mustard
1 T. brown sugar

Mix first 7 ingredients together well and divide into 5 round loaves. Cook at 350° for 40-50 minutes. Mix together remaining 3 ingredients to make a sauce. Put sauce on top of loaves and cook for another 10 minutes.

Grandma's Barese Pizza

Melissa Cosenza   *Italy*

40 minutes to bake
Makes 20 2x2" pieces

4-5 medium potatoes
1/4 lb. baker's yeast
1/2 t. salt
6 c. flour
water (if necessary)
4 T. olive oil
1 c. tomato sauce
1/4 t. black ground pepper
1/2 t. oregano
1/2 lb. mozzarella, thinly sliced

Preheat oven to 375°. Peel and boil potatoes until they
break when a fork is inserted. Mash on an open, large surface. Sprinkle 1/4 t. salt and crumble yeast onto potatoes.
Mash together. Add flour gradually. Knead easily and do not
overwork. Discard small pieces of dough that are not
joining the cohesive ball. If the dough is dry, add a couple
of tablespoons of cool water. Evenly coat the dough with
flour. The coating will break and crack as the dough grows.
Let it rise for one hour or until it doubles in size under a
dish towel on a flat surface. This makes one large pizza or if
more potatoes and flour are used, two smaller ones. Adjust
the recipe to your taste.

Place dough in a 13" x 9" x 2" pan coated with olive oil.
Spread dough until it is 3/4" thick all around and oval in
shape. Pour tomato sauce on center of pizza. Spread thinly
and evenly with a spoon and leave a 1" crust. Sprinkle
remainder of salt, pepper, and oregano on pizza. Place in
375° oven for 40 minutes or until golden brown on sides
and bottom. Remove and place mozzarella on as desired.
Other toppings are optional and should be placed under
cheese. Place pizza back into oven to melt cheese. Serve
warm.

Chicken Breasts

Jane Birnbaum

Makes 4-6 servings
One hour to bake; marinate overnight

4 whole chicken breasts
2 cloves garlic, minced
2 t. ginger
1 t. oregano
2 T. brown sugar
1/2 c. soy sauce
1 c. wine

Mix ingredients and pour over chicken. Allow to marinate overnight or several hours in refrigerator. Seal baking dish with foil and bake for 1 hour at 375°. Serve with rice.

The previous New York City House on 86th Street could house only 26 families (compared with the present 84 at our new House on East 73rd Street) and 30 to 40 families were turned away every week.

Pastas

Rigatoni with Tomatoes and Vodka

Loretta Scomillio   *Italy*

Makes 4 servings
30 minutes to prepare

2 T. butter
1 small onion, chopped
2 cloves garlic, minced
1 T. dried Italian seasonings, crumbled
1 16 oz. can Italian plum tomatoes, chopped, juices reserved
3 oz. sliced prosciutto or ham, chopped
1/2 c. vodka
3/4 c. whipping cream
1 c. grated parmesan cheese
8 oz. rigatoni or other tubular pasta, freshly cooked

Melt butter in a heavy skillet over medium-high heat. Add onion, garlic, and Italian seasonings and sauté until onion is translucent, about 4 minutes. Add tomatoes, reserved juices, and prosciutto and simmer for 10 minutes, stirring occasionally. Add vodka and simmer for 5 minutes. Add cream and 1/2 c. parmesan cheese. Simmer until sauce thickens slightly, about 4 minutes. Add rigatoni and stir until sauce coats pasta. Season with salt and pepper. Serve, passing remaining 1/2 c. parmesan cheese separately.

Garlic Shrimp Pasta

Bari Goldsmith   *United States*

20 minutes to prepare

1-2 lbs. cooked and peeled shrimp, fresh or frozen
1 container Contadina pesto sauce
1 small can tomato sauce
1 lb. fresh linguine
olive oil

Sauté shrimp in oil until warm. Add pesto sauce and tomato sauce; simmer for 10 minutes. Serve over a bed of cooked linguine.

Herb Pasta with Butter, Cheese, and Cream

Michele Schaechter

15 minutes to prepare

8 T. butter
1 c. heavy cream
1 lb. fresh herb-specked pasta
1 c. grated parmesan cheese
salt
freshly ground pepper
pinch of ground nutmeg

In a heavy casserole, over direct heat, combine butter and half of the cream. Over low heat, simmer until the butter and cream have melted. Turn off the heat. Separately cook pasta for a minute or so, drain well, and add to the casserole with the butter and cream. Turn on heat under casserole and, with two spoons, lift and toss the pasta, coating completely. Add the remaining cream, parmesan cheese, salt, pepper, and nutmeg. Toss briefly again. Serve immediately with grated cheese on the side.

Lasagna Roll-ups

Lori Thaler   *United States*

8 lasagna noodles
1 T. olive oil
2 large cloves garlic, minced
1 10 oz. pkg. chopped spinach, thawed and well drained
1 c. ricotta cheese
1 t. salt
1 c. shredded mozzarella
1 14 oz. jar spaghetti sauce

Prepare lasagna noodles as package directs; drain and lay flat until ready to use. Meanwhile, heat oil in 12" skillet over medium flame and sauté garlic 2 minutes or just until tender, stirring frequently.

In a medium size bowl, combine spinach, ricotta, garlic and 1/2 the mozzarella. Spread each coated lasagna noodle with a heaping 1/4 c. of spinach mixture. Roll up firmly, jelly-roll fashion.

Pour spaghetti sauce into 12" skillet. Place rolls seam-side down in skillet. Bring to a boil. Reduce heat to low. Cover and simmer 5 minutes. Sprinkle on the remaining mozzarella. Cover and simmer 3 to 5 minutes, or until rolls are heated through.

Lisa's Linguine with White Clam Sauce

Lisa Gandal

15 minutes to prepare

1 lb. linguine
2 cans minced clams
1 t. butter
4-5 cloves garlic, minced
Juice of 1/4 lemon
2 T. white wine
oil
salt
pepper
parmesan cheese

In a saucepan, fry garlic in oil. Add clams and clam juice and cook on low heat. Add lemon juice, wine, salt, pepper, and butter. Simmer until warm. Toss with linguine; top with parmesan.

Lemon and Red Pepper Pasta

Julie Huh

Pasta:
2 T. butter
1 sweet red pepper
1 lemon
1 c. heavy cream
salt, black pepper, cayenne pepper
1/2 lb. fresh fresh fettuccini
grated Parmesan cheese

Veal scallops:
1 lb. veal scallops
2 lemons
1 c. fresh bread crumbs
1/2 c. grated parmesan cheese
salt and black pepper
1 egg
4 T. butter
2 T. olive oil
1 T. chopped parsley
1 lemon rind

Combine butter, pepper and lemon (juice and rind) into a skillet. Add cream and salt and pepper. Boil pasta, add to cream sauce, and combine with veal when cooked.

To make lemon veal scallops, mix crumbs, cheese, and seasonings. Beat egg and 2 T. of lemon juice. Dip each scallop in egg mixture, then in crumb mixture. Saute scallops in a large skillet about 30 seconds each side.

Lasagna

Andrea Tashjian   *Italy*

Makes 12 servings
60 to 90 minutes to bake

2 boxes lasagna
2 (12 oz.) containers ricotta cheese
2 eggs, beaten
2 large jars tomato sauce
1 large pkg. mozzarella cheese
oregano (optional)

Mix ricotta cheese and eggs. Layer the lasagna pan as follows: tomato sauce, noodles (uncooked), cheese and egg mixture, sliced mozzarella. Repeat for 3 layers and top with mozzarella and sauce.

Bake at 350° for 60-90 minutes in large pan.

Brocachini Lasagna

Linda Huss

20 minutes to prepare

1 lb. rigatoni
1 head broccoli
3 eggs
6-8 slices of bacon
1 pint light cream
10 oz. sharp Italian cheese
1 stick butter

Mix eggs and cream in a large bowl. Cook bacon and crumble into mixture. Melt butter and grate cheese, then set them aside.

Cook pasta, drain water, and immediately pour in bowl over mixture. Add butter and cheese. Toss until thoroughly melted.

Mom's Macaroni and Cheese Lasagna

Linda Huss

Makes 4 servings

1/2 lb. elbow macaroni
2 c. shredded sharp cheddar cheese
butter or margarine
salt and pepper to taste
milk

Cook macaroni in a 1-qt. saucepan with salted water
approximately 10 minutes or until tender. Drain well.

In a well-buttered casserole dish, layer macaroni, cheese,
dabs of butter, salt, and pepper into three layers. Pour
enough milk over the mixture to cover well. Bake for 45 to
60 minutes at 350°.

Bacon Browned Vermicelli Lasagna

Virginia Brown   *Italy*

Makes 4-6 servings
30 minutes to prepare

4-6 slices thick bacon, chopped
1 pkg. (8 oz.) vermicelli or thin spaghetti
1 pkg. (8 oz.) fresh mushrooms, sliced
1 medium onion, chopped
1 1/4 c. hot water
1 T. chicken flavored bouillon
dash of hot sauce

In a large skillet, cook bacon until crisp. Remove and set aside. Drain all but 1/4 cup of drippings.

Add uncooked vermicelli, onion, and mushrooms to skillet. Cook and stir until vermicelli is browned. Stir in water, bouillon, and hot sauce. Cover and cook on low for 10-12 minutes, stirring often. Add bacon and toss well. Serve immediately.

Rigatoni Avodka

Marilyn Cote

1 lb. rigatoni
1/2 c. heavy cream
1/2 c. sour cream
1/2 stick butter or margarine
1 1/2 shots vodka
1/2 c. grated cheese
pepper to taste
1 1/2 c. tomato sauce

While pasta is cooking, melt butter in medium pan and add vodka. Burn off vodka (allow it to evaporate).

Mix sour and heavy cream together, then add to butter and vodka. Stir together. Cook about 2 minutes.

Drain pasta and toss with vodka sauce. Then toss with tomato sauce. Finally sprinkle with grated cheese.

Linguine with Tomatoes and Basil

Kate Merchant   *Italy*

Makes 4-6 servings

4 ripe large tomatoes, cut into 1/2" cubes
1 lb. brie cheese, rind removed, torn into irregular pieces
1 c. cleaned, fresh basil leaves, cut into strips
3 cloves garlic, peeled and finely minced
1 c. plus 1 T. best quality olive oil
2 1/2 t. salt
1/2 t. freshly ground black pepper
1 1/2 lbs. linguine
freshly grated parmesan cheese
sun-dried tomatoes

Combine tomatoes, brie, basil, garlic, 1 c. olive oil, 1/2 t. salt and pepper in a large serving bowl. Prepare at least 2 hours before serving. Cover and set aside at room temperature.

Bring 6 quarts of water to a boil in a large pot. Add 1 T. olive oil and remaining salt. Add the linguine and boil until tender but still firm (about 8-10 minutes).

Drain pasta and immediately toss with the tomato sauce. Serve at once, passing the pepper mill and grated parmesan cheese and sun-dried tomatoes.

Vegetables &
Side Dishes

Oriental Rice

Susan Birnbaum   *China*

25 minutes to prepare

1/4 lb. diced onion
1 t. sesame oil
1/2 c. long grain rice
1 c. chicken stock
1 t. reduced-sodium soy sauce

Sauté onion in hot sesame oil in heavy pot for a few minutes until onion softens and browns. Add rice, stock, and soy sauce. Bring to a boil. Reduce heat, cover, and simmer until rice is tender and liquid has been absorbed, about 17 minutes.

Chaahan (Japanese Style Fried Rice)

Japan

6 c. cold steamed rice
1 1/2 c. chopped onion
1 c. chopped carrot
1 c. chopped green pepper
1 c. corn
1 lb. ground beef
soy sauce
1 stump broccoli
2 cloves chopped garlic
2 eggs

Soak beef in a little soy sauce for about 30 minutes.

Make scrambled eggs in a separate pan. Put about 1 T. oil in a heated pan. Add chopped garlic when oil is hot; stir until garlic browns. Put all vegetables in pan and fry. Add salt and pepper as desired. When vegetables are almost done, pour rice into pan. Add sesame oil if desired. Add scrambled eggs and 1 T. soy sauce. Fry well together.

Rice Pilaf

Marina Peredo

Makes 4-6 servings

2 c. enriched, long grain rice
1 1/2 c. minced onion
1 1/2 c. grated carrots
1 lb. boneless meat chunks, lamb or chicken
4 c. water
1 t. salt
1 t. paprika
1 t. chili powder
1 t. corn oil

In a frying pan, heat 1 t. corn oil and sauté meat pieces until they brown lightly (about 10 minutes). Remove and set aside.

Heat the oil and sauté the onions until golden. Mix the meat and onions together and sauté for 10 minutes. Transfer the mixture into a large saucepan. Add carrots to the top, cover, and let simmer for 5 minutes. Mix everything together and add salt.

Add rice on top of the mixture. Pour the presalted water slowly into the saucepan. Add paprika and chili powder. Cook uncovered until the water barely covers the rice, then cover and continue to cook another 5 minutes. Remove the lid and cook over low heat until the water evaporates. Mix together.

Broccoli, Rice, Cheese Casserole

Mary Luca

1 hour to bake

2 (8 oz.) pkgs. frozen chopped broccoli
2 c. water
2 cans cream of mushroom soup
1 stick salted butter
2 c. minute rice
1 (6 oz.) jar processed cheese spread

Combine ingredients in a 9" x 13" pan. Bake uncovered for 30 minutes at 350°. Remove from oven, stir, and bake another 30 minutes.

Peperonats (braised sweet peppers with tomatoes and onions)

Lucille Buyko   *Italy*

Makes 4-6 servings
25 to 30 minutes to prepare

2 T. butter
1/4 c. olive oil
1 lb. onions, sliced 1/8" thick
2 lbs. green and red peppers, seeded and cut
   into 1/2" strips
2 lbs. tomatoes, coarsely chopped
1 t. red wine vinegar
1 t. freshly ground black pepper

In a heavy 12" skillet, melt butter with the oil, and add the onions. Cook, turning them frequently for 10 minutes, until soft and lightly browned. Stir in the peppers, reduce heat, cover and cook for 10 minutes. Add tomatoes, vinegar, salt and black pepper and cook covered for another 5 minutes.

Then cook uncovered, on high heat, stirring gently until almost all of the liquid has boiled away. Serve as a hot vegetable dish or chill and serve cold as an antipasto or as an accompaniment to roast meats or fowl. Great with fried or charcoal Italian sausage.

Quiche

Kathryn Childs

45 minutes to bake

homemade or pre-prepared 9" pie crust (un-cooked)
8 slices bacon, cooked and crumbled
6 oz. Swiss cheese (grated)
3 eggs
1 c. heavy cream
1/2 c. milk
1/2 t. salt
1/2 t. dried mustard
1/4 t. pepper
cayenne pepper

Put bacon and cheese in pie crust. In a separate bowl, add the eggs, cream, milk, salt, mustard, and pepper. Beat together and pour over bacon and cheese. Sprinkle with a dash of cayenne pepper. Bake at 375° for 45 minutes or until knife stuck in center comes out clean.

Broccoli Casserole

Carmela Altieri

Makes 8 servings
10 minutes to prepare; 20-30 minutes to bake; 10 minutes to
  set

2 boxes frozen broccoli
1 egg
pepper
1 T. minced onion
1/2 c. mayonnaise
1 can cream of mushroom or golden mushroom soup
1 pkg. shredded cheddar cheese
cornflake or bread crumbs
shortening spray

Thaw or cook lightly the broccoli, and drain. In the meanwhile, beat 1 egg. Combine all other ingredients and the
broccoli and egg, except the crumbs and spray. Pour into a
greased 1-qt. casserole. Top with crumbs. Spray crumbs
lightly with shortening spray to coat and give crispiness
when baked.

Bake in a preheated medium oven (250-300°) for about
20-30 minutes (when sides lightly bubble or when crumbs
brown). Remove and let set for 10 minutes.

Broccoli Souffle

Sofia Parish

40-55 minutes to bake

9" pie shell
3 T. flour
2 T. mayonnaise
1 pkg. onion soup mix
2 pkgs. chopped broccoli, drained
3 eggs
4 T. margarine

Mix all ingredients and pour into pie shell. Bake at 350° for 40-55 minutes. An 8" x 8" pan can also be used instead of pie shell.

The donations raised by caring people all over the world help keep the daily cost for a family's stay at the Ronald McDonald House at $20.

Curried Broccoli or Cauliflower Casserole

Marianna Rotondo   *India*

30 minutes to bake

1 large head of broccoli or cauliflower, broken into pieces,
*   boiled, and drained*
1 can cream of mushroom soup
1 c. grated cheddar cheese
1/3 c. mayonnaise
1 t. curry powder
1/4 c. bread crumbs
2 T. butter or margarine

Place cooked vegetable in 2-qt. casserole. Blend cream of mushroom soup, cheese, mayonnaise, and curry powder. Pour over vegetable, toss lightly to coat.

Combine bread crumbs with butter. Sprinkle over mixture. Bake for 30 minutes at 350°.

Three-Onion Casserole

Susan Durtschi   *United States*

Makes 6 servings
20 minutes to mix; 1 hour to bake

3 T. butter
2 large yellow onions, thinly sliced
2 large red onions, thinly sliced
4 medium leeks, well-rinsed, dried, and thinly sliced
1 1/2 c. grated Havarti cheese
2 pkg. (5 oz. each) Boursin with herb cheese
1 1/2 c. Gruyere cheese, grated
1/2 c. dry white wine

Pre-heat oven to 350°. Grease 8-cup baking dish with 1 T.
butter. Layer onions and leeks on the bottom of dish.
Sprinkle with salt and pepper. Top with Havarti and make
another layer of onions and leeks. Top with Boursin cheese.
Layer remaining onions and leeks and top with Gruyere. Dot
with 2 T. butter. Pour wine over casserole.

Bake for 1 hour. Cover if it becomes too brown.

Fried Rice

Barbara Seipt

Makes 4 servings
35 minutes to prepare

2 T. salad oil
1 bunch scallions
2 c. cooked rice
salt to taste
1 c. chopped celery
2 T. soy sauce
1 pkg. chopped, roasted almonds

Sauté scallions and celery in oil until glassy, not brown. Add rice, salt, and soy sauce.

Mix and place in casserole dish. Bake at 350° for 25-30 minutes. Toss almonds on top just before serving.

Potato Cakes

Eileen Moore   *Ireland*

Makes 6 servings
20 minutes to prepare

2 lbs. potatoes
1/2 lb. ham
1 egg
2 onions
1 c. flour
salt and pepper

Peel, boil, and mash potatoes. Cut ham into pieces and chop onions. Add to the potatoes.

Beat egg in a bowl. Put flour, salt, and pepper in a separate bowl. Make potato mixture into patties. Dip into egg and dredge into flour. Put in pan and fry for approximately 5 minutes or until brown. Serve hot with butter.

Spinach Stuffed Tomatoes

Millie Dent   *England*

Makes 6 servings

2 pkgs. frozen, chopped spinach
1 large pkg. cream cheese
1 t. salt
pinch of nutmeg
freshly ground pepper
6 large hollowed tomatoes

Cook spinach according to directions. Drain thoroughly and add cream cheese, salt, nutmeg, and pepper. Blend until thoroughly mixed and add seasonings to taste.

Stuff mixture into tomato shells and cook at 350° for 30 minutes.

Zucchini Bake

Lela Rotondo   *Italy*

45 minutes to bake

3 c. zucchini, cubed
1/2 c. Bisquick
1/2 c. oil
1 medium onion, chopped

4 eggs
salt and pepper
1 c. cheddar cheese,
  shredded

Pre-heat oven to 350°. Grease a round pan or flan pan. Mix all ingredients until well blended. Bake for about 45 minutes or until golden brown on top.

Sweet Potato Medallions

Caron Kass   *United States*

6 medium sweet potatoes
2 medium apples
3/4 c. packed brown sugar
1/4 c. melted butter
1/4 t. ginger
1/4 t. nutmeg
1/4 t. cinnamon
1/4 c. flaky coconut
Optional: bag of small marshmallows

Peel and slice potatoes into 1/4" pieces. Cook covered in 2 inches boiling salted water for 10 minutes or until almost tender. Drain. Peel and core apples. Combine brown sugar, butter, ginger, nutmeg and cinnamon in a 10" x 6" x 2" baking dish.

Layer one-third of potatoes, one-half of apples, and 2 T. of brown sugar mixture over apples. Repeat layers again. Arrange remaining potatoes and brown mixture in the pan.

Bake covered at 325° for 40 minutes. Uncover and sprinkle coconut over the top. Bake uncovered for 15 more minutes. Optional: sprinkle marshmallows over the top.

Saucy Cheese Bake

Melissa Napolitano   *United States*

Makes 4 servings
25 minutes to bake

8 oz. Pennsylvania Dutch egg noodles
1 lb. ground beef
2 (15 oz.) cans of tomato sauce
1/2 c. chopped onion
1 T. chopped parsley
1/4 t. basil
1/4 t. garlic powder
1/4 t. oregano
3 c. shredded cheddar cheese

Preheat oven to 350°. Cook noodles according to pkg. directions. Brown beef in skillet and drain fat. Stir in tomato sauce, onion, parsley, basil, garlic powder, and oregano. Simmer, stirring occasionally for 15 minutes.

In a 3-qt. oblong baking dish, layer 1/2 sauce, noodles, then cheese; repeat, ending with cheese. Bake for 25 minutes or until heated through. Cover dish with foil until last 5 minutes of baking time or noodles will harden.

Vegetarian Rice Bake

Claudia T. Rodriguez   *United States*

Makes 2 servings
45 minutes to bake

1 can (8 oz.) whole tomatoes
1 can (8 3/4 oz.) kidney beans, drained
1/2 c. rice
2/3 c. sliced zucchini
1/2 c. chopped onion
1 t. chili powder
3/4 t. cumin
1/4 t. garlic salt
1/4 c. green, red, or yellow pepper strips
1/4 c.- 1/2 c. shredded low-moisture, part-skim mozzarella
   cheese, depending on taste

Drain and chop tomatoes, reserving juice. Add enough
water to juice to equal 1 1/3 cups.

Combine tomatoes, tomato liquid, and next 7 ingredients
in 8-inch square baking dish; mix well. Cover tightly with
foil. Bake at 350° for 45 minutes or until most of the liquid is
absorbed. Uncover and stir. Sprinkle peppers and cheese
over top. Return to oven until cheese is melted.

Stuffing Balls

Barbara L. Bush　　　　　*United States*

Makes 6 servings

4 c. chopped celery & leaves
2 large onions, chopped
2 t. thyme
2 t. sage
1 t. salt
1/2 t. pepper
1/2 c. margarine
1 c. chicken broth or water
8 c. soft, stale bread crumbs

Sauté celery, onions, seasonings in margarine in a skillet for 5 minutes. Add remaining ingredients and mix well.

Shape into 12 balls and put one in each of 12 well-greased muffin pan sections. Bake at 350° for 30 minutes.

Last year, the Ronald McDonald House of NYC served families from 36 states and 45 foreign countries.

Baked Beans

Jackie Russell   *United States*

70 minutes to bake

3/4 lb. bacon; about 18 slices, diced
3 medium onions, chopped
1 t. garlic powder
1/2 t. dried mustard
3/4 c. brown sugar
1/4 c. ketchup
1/2 c. cider vinegar
1 (15 1/2 oz.) can kidney beans, drained (light or dark red)
1 (15 1/2 oz.) can butter beans, drained
2 (21 oz.) cans pork and beans (try B&B)

Sauté bacon and onions in a pot until soft; drain. Combine the rest of the ingredients, mix with bacon and onions, and bake uncovered in a 350° oven for about 1 hour and 10 minutes until hot and bubbly.

Quick and Healthy Quiche

Makes 4 servings
40 minutes to bake

1 deep dish frozen pie crust
1/2 pint heavy cream
3 eggs
1 c. grated swiss cheese
"Goodies" (mushrooms, artichokes, capers, tomatoes,
   spinach, broccoli,etc...)
nutmeg

In a bowl, beat together heavy cream and eggs.

Let pie shell come to room temperature and poke fork holes in the bottom. Add "goodies" of your choice (well drained) and sprinkle with grated cheese. Pour beaten heavy cream and eggs over the top. Sprinkle with nutmeg. Bake at 375° for 25 minutes, then at 325° for 15 more minutes.

Baked Cheese Garlic Grits

Melissa Napolitano   *Southern United States*

Makes 4-6 servings

3 c. water
3/4 c. Quickgrits
1/4 t. salt
1 c. shredded cheddar cheese
2 T. margarine
1 egg, beaten
1/8 t. garlic powder

Heat oven to 350°. Grease 1 1/2 qt. baking dish. Prepare grits according to package directions. Stir in remaining ingredients. Continue cooking over low heat until cheese is melted. Pour into prepared dish and bake 30 minutes. Let stand 5 minutes before serving.

Desserts

Easy Cheese Cake

Mom   *Italy*

Makes 8 servings
1 hour to prepare

1 lb. cream cheese
3 eggs
2/3 c. sugar
1/2 t. almond extract

Beat softened cream cheese and sugar. Add eggs and almond extract. Beat until smooth, thick, and lemon-colored. Pour into a greased 9" pie plate. Bake at 350° about 30 minutes, or until it puffs up. Remove from oven and cool for 20 minutes.

For a topping, combine 1 t. vanilla, 1 c. sour cream and 3 T. sugar. Heat well. Pour over top and bake at 350° for an additional 10 minutes. Cool and enjoy.

Chocolate Chip Cookies

Annalisa   *United States*

Makes 4 dozen cookies
10-12 minutes to bake

1 c. + 2 T. sifted all-purpose flour
1/2 t. baking soda
1/2 t. salt
1/2 c. granulated sugar
1/4 c. light brown sugar, firmly packed
1 egg
1 t. vanilla extract
1/2 c. soft butter or margarine
1/2 c. coarsely chopped walnuts or pecans
1 pkg. (6 oz.) semi-sweet chocolate pieces

Preheat oven to 375°. Into a large bowl, sift flour with baking soda and salt. Add sugar, eggs, vanilla, and butter. With
a wooden spoon or portable electric mixer at medium
speed, beat until smooth and well combined, about 1
minute.

Stir in nuts and chocolate pieces. Drop by the teaspoon-
ful, 2 inches apart, onto ungreased cookie sheets. Bake 10-
12 minutes, or until golden. Remove, place on wire rack and
let cool.

No Bake Cheesecake

Maria Restieri

Makes 8 slices
10 minutes to prepare; 4 hours to set

1 Graham cracker pie crust
1 pkg. (8 oz.) cream cheese,
   softened
1 8 oz. container Cool Whip
fresh fruit: blueberries, strawberries,
   or 1 can cherry pie filling

1 c. sour cream
2 t. vanilla
1/3 c. sugar

Beat cheese until smooth; gradually beat in sugar. Blend in sour cream and vanilla. Fold in whipped topping, blending well. Spoon into crust. Garnish with fruit. Chill and let set at least four hours.

Sarasota Opera Society Chocolate Cake

Christa Piccione   *United States*

Makes 12-16 servings
15 minutes to mix; 1 hour to prepare

1 pkg. devil's food cake mix
1 (3 oz.) pkg. chocolate or fudge instant pudding
3/4 c. oil
1 c. sour cream
4 large eggs
6 oz. chocolate chips
1 T. instant coffee

Combine all ingredients except chips in a large bowl. Beat slowly at first, then at high speed for 2 minutes.

Fold in chips. Bake at 350° for 1 hour in a greased and floured 10" tube or bundt pan. Cool completely before removing from pan.

Easy Pound Cake

Mary Cicorelli

30 minutes to bake

1 1/2 c. Presto flour
1 c. sugar
1/2 pint heavy cream
2 eggs
1 t. vanilla

Place all ingredients into a bowl. Beat for 2 minutes. Place batter in a greased, wax paper-lined loaf pan. Bake at 350° for 30 minutes or until toothpick comes out clean.

Frozen Mandarins

Marianne Huss   *Japan*

Makes 4 servings

4 mandarin oranges
orange sherbet
sugar wafers
orange-flavored liqueur

Thoroughly wet unpeeled oranges with water and put them in the freezer overnight.

When ready to serve, peel back mandarin skin in flower-like pattern, but do not remove entirely.

Place mandarin "flower" on top of crushed ice in a bowl and top fruit with a bit of orange flavored liqueur. Then place a scoop of orange sherbet on top of fruit. Serve with sugar wafer and chilled spoon.

After sherbet is eaten, guests pick apart frozen fruit that melts in their mouths.

Frozen Lemon Mousse

Jeanie B. Riegel

Makes 12 servings
15 minutes to mix; 8 hours to freeze

30 lemon or vanilla wafers
4 egg yolks
1/2 c. fresh lemon juice
1/4 c. sugar
1 1/2 T. grated lemon zest
4 egg whites
1/8 t. cream of tartar
1/8 t. salt
3/4 c. sugar
1 1/2 c. whipping cream

Line the bottom and sides of an 8-9" inch springform pan with wafers. Combine the next four ingredients in a large bowl and blend well. Let stand at room temperature.

Beat the egg whites until foamy. Add cream of tartar and salt and continue beating until soft peaks form. Gradually add remaining sugar, beating constantly until stiff and glossy.

Whip cream until stiff. Gently fold whites and cream into yolk mixture. Carefully spoon into pan. Cover with foil and freeze at least eight hours.

Let soften in the refrigerator one hour before serving.

Seven Layer Cookies

Jeanie B. Riegel

15 minutes to mix; 30 minutes to bake

1 stick margarine
1 c. graham cracker crumbs
1 can Eagle Brand condensed milk
1 pkg. (6 oz.) chocolate bits
1 pkg. (6 oz.) butterscotch bits
1 small can Angle Flake coconut
1 c. pecan or almond pieces

Melt margarine in a 9" x 11" pan. Add graham cracker crumbs, spreading evenly over margarine.

Spread coconut over mixture. Next add chocolate bits, butterscotch bits, nuts, and lastly, pour milk over all.

Bake at 350° for 30 minutes. Top with whipped cream if desired.

The Ronald McDonald House works with 12 major hospitals in New York City.

Cheesecake

Teresa Notari   *Italy/United States*

Makes 8-10 servings
3 hours to prepare

2 (8 oz.) pkgs. cream cheese
15 oz. ricotta cheese
4 eggs
1 1/2 c. sugar
3 T. flour
3 T. cornstarch
1 1/2 T. lemon juice
1 t. vanilla
1 pint sour cream
1 stick margarine or butter

Grease and flour a 9" springform pan. Preheat oven to 350°.
Combine all ingredients well and pour into pan.

Bake for 1 hour. Turn oven off and leave in for another
hour. Do not open oven door during these 2 hours! Take
out of oven and wait 20 minutes before unlocking springform pan.

Apple Pandowdy

Stasia Finkelstein

Makes 6-8 servings
15 minutes to prepare; 30 minutes to bake

6 large apples
1 c. flour
1 t. baking powder
1/2 t. salt
1 egg
3 T. Crisco shortening
brown sugar
sugar
cinnamon

Grease a baking dish with butter and fill halfway with peeled and sliced apples. Cover with white sugar and a little butter. Add the rest of the apples and top with more white sugar and brown sugar.

Mix all of the other ingredients, except cinnamon, in a bowl, stir until thick, and spread on top. Sprinkle with cinnamon.

Bake at 350° for 30 minutes or until brown. Serve plain, with ice cream, or with heavy cream.

Dravle (caramel pudding)

Nordic Delicacies Inc.　　*Norway*

Makes 8 servings
15 minutes to mix; around 4 hours to cook

2 quarts whole milk
2 eggs, slightly beaten
1 c. dairy sour cream
1 T. all-purpose flour
1/2 c. sugar
1/2 c. chopped walnuts

Pour milk into a heavy 4-qt. saucepan. Stirring constantly, bring to a boil over medium-low heat. Reduce heat to lowest possible setting. Stirring occasionally, simmer 3 to 4 hours, or until the milk is reduced to about 4 cups and has a light tan color.

In a small bowl, blend eggs, sour cream, flour, and sugar. Stir 1/2 cup hot milk into egg mixture. Stir egg mixture into remaining hot milk. Cook and stir over low heat until mixture is thickened and slightly curdled (about 10 minutes). Serve hot, sprinkled with walnuts.

Applesauce Pie

Linda Huss   *United States*

Approximately 10 minutes to mix; 1 hour to bake;
2 hours to chill

1 graham cracker pie crust
1 24-25 oz. jar of applesauce
1 T. flour
2 T. white sugar
2 T. brown sugar (add sugars if applesauce is unsweetened)

The following ingredients are optional:
1 t. cinnamon
1/2 t. nutmeg
1/2 t. ginger
1/2 t. salt
graham cracker or ginger snap crumbs

Combine applesauce, flour, white and brown sugar (if sauce
is unsweetened), and all of the other ingredients. Sprinkle
graham cracker or ginger snap crumbs on top, if desired.
   Bake at 300-325° for 1 hour. Chill for 2 hours.

Cinnamon Topped Coffee Cake

Barbara Seipt

10 minutes to mix; 20-25 minutes to bake

Cake:
1 c. sugar
3 T. butter
1 egg
2 c. flour
1 1/3 T. baking powder
1 t. salt
1 c. milk
1 t. vanilla

Topping:
1 c. sugar
1/2 c. flour
1 T. butter
1 T. cinnamon

Cake: Cream together sugar, butter, and egg. Sift together the dry ingredients. Add wet (milk and vanilla) and dry ingredients alternately to sugar mixture.

Topping: Mix butter with other ingredients and put on top of cake batter before baking.

Bake at 350° for 20-25 minutes.

Death By Chocolate

Beth Shubert

Makes 10-15 servings

1 very deep trifle dish
1 c. Kahlua liqueur
4 boxes of Jello brand instant chocolate mousse
4 cups of milk (for the mousse)
6 Skor candy bars, crushed
2 tubs Cool Whip, or real whipped cream
1 box of chocolate/devil's food cake mix

Prepare and bake cake. Let cool. Pierce surface of cake all over with a fork. Pour liqueur over surface. Cover pan with foil or plastic and chill overnight.

The next day, prepare the mousse (follow the directions on the box) in a deep bowl, and chill for 2 hours.

To assemble everything: Chop cake into 1 inch pieces and layer about 1/2 of it in the bottom of the trifle dish. Add a layer of mousse (about 1/2). Sprinkle about 1/3 of the candy over the mousse. Layer about 1/2 of the Cool Whip. Repeat the layering, ending with the Cool Whip, and sprinkle the remaining candy on top.

Chill the assembled dish for 1 to 10 hours.

Sherry Trifle

Eileen Moore   *Ireland*

Makes 12 servings

1 pound cake, sliced
2 cans of fruit cocktail
1 banana
2 pkgs. red Jello gelatin
1/2 glass of sherry
1 pint cream

In a foil tray, soak pound cake in sherry for 5 minutes. Drain fruit cocktail and add to the pound cake mixture. Prepare two packages of Jello and add to mixture. Add banana to mixture and leave to set overnight in refrigerator. Serve with whipped cream.

Easy Banana Bread

Wendy Cohen

10 minutes to mix; 1 hour to bake

3 bananas, mashed
1 c. sugar
1/2 c. margarine (softened)
2 eggs
2 c. flour
1 T. baking soda
1 t. salt
1/2 c. chopped walnuts (optional)

Mix together all of the ingredients. Put into a greased and floured pan. Bake at 325° for 1 hour.

Thin Batter-Fresh Fruit Cake

Ethel Dosso

15 minutes to prepare; 35 minutes to bake

1 1/4 c. Presto cake flour
1 egg, beaten
4 T. melted butter or margarine
peaches, plums, or apples
3/4 c. sugar, granulated
powdered sugar for top of cake
pinch of salt
1/4 c. milk

Sift flour and add sugar and salt. Add egg and melted butter; mix with milk. Mix together in a bowl with a fork. The batter should be thick enough to spread with a knife.

Butter a 13" x 10" baking pan. Spread the batter in a pan.

Cut fresh fruit in quartered slices and make rows of fruit on top of batter and sprinkle with granulated sugar.

Bake until brown and bubbly (about 35 minutes at 350°). When cool, sift powdered sugar on top.

Peanut Butter Kiss Cookies

Fran Wallach

15 minutes to prepare; 12 minutes to bake

18 oz. creamy peanut butter
2 eggs
1 to 1 1/4 c. sugar
9 oz. pkg. of Hershey Kisses

Mix peanut butter, sugar, and eggs together. Roll into balls (about 1 1/2" diameter) and place on a cookie sheet.

Bake 10-12 minutes at 350°.

Remove cookies from oven and place a Hershey Kiss in the middle of each cookie.

Pralines

Nora Falk

6-7 minutes to cook

1 pkg. light brown sugar
4-6 T. water
1/8 lb. butter
1 can pecans (halves)

Cook sugar, water, butter together for about 6-7 minutes until soft ball forms. Remove from heat, add pecans and immediately spoon out onto waxed paper.

Wrap in wax paper to store.

Frozen Toffee Cream Pie

1 1/2 c. chocolate wafer crumbs
6 T. butter, melted
1 c. whipping cream
2/3 c. sweetened condensed milk
1/4 c. strong coffee
1/2 t. vanilla
2-3 Heath bars, crushed

Combine chocolate wafer crumbs and butter (crust must be homemade to be good); press firmly in a 9" pie plate. Chill.

Meanwhile, in a small mixer bowl combine cream, condensed milk, coffee, and vanilla on low speed electric mixer. Then beat on high speed about 4 minutes or until thickened.

Reserve 2 T. of the Heath bars (or more) and stir the remaining into the cream mixture. Pour into crumb crust. Sprinkle with the reserved Heath bar.

Freeze until firm, several hours or overnight.

Oatmeal Raisin Cookies

30 minutes to make

2 c. flour
1 1/4 c. sugar
1 t. baking powder
1/2 t. baking soda
1 t. salt and cinnamon
3 c. oats
1 c. raisins
1 c. oil
2 eggs
1/2 c. milk

Combine all of the ingredients well. Bake 10-12 minutes at 400°.

Margies's Chef Cookies

12 to 15 minutes to bake

2 eggs
1 c. margarine (2 sticks)
1 c. sugar
2 t. vanilla
1 c. brown sugar (dark)
2 1/2 c. oatmeal
2 c. flour
1 t. salt
1 t. baking soda
1 t. baking powder
1 (12 oz.) bag of chocolate chips
1 1/2 c. chopped walnuts

In a bowl, mix eggs, margarine, sugar, vanilla, and brown sugar. Add in oatmeal, flour, salt, baking soda, baking powder, chocolate chips, and chopped walnuts.

Shape into golf ball size balls. Bake 12-15 minutes at 350°.

Cranberry Mousse

Cynthia White   *United States*

Makes 8 servings

1 c. Ocean Spray Cranberry juice cocktail
1 pkg. (4 serving size) raspberry Jello flavor gelatin, or
   sugar-free
1 can (16 oz.) Ocean Spray CranRaspberry sauce
2 c. thawed non-dairy whipped topping

Heat cranberry juice cocktail to boiling. Remove from heat.
Stir in gelatin until dissolved.

Beat cranberry raspberry sauce with electric beater on
high speed for 1 minute; stir into gelatin mixture. Chill until
thickened, about 2 1/2 hours.

Fold in whipped topping, blend thoroughly. Spoon into
dessert dishes or prepared 9" pie shell. Chill until firm, at
least 3 hours. CranRaspberry juice can be substituted for
CranRaspberry sauce.

Julgrot (Christmas rice pudding)

Nordic Delicacies Inc.   Scandinavia

Makes 8-12 servings

3/4 c. medium-grain rice, uncooked
1/2 t. salt
1 1/2 c. boiling water
2 c. whipping cream
2 c. milk
2 eggs, beaten
5/6 c. sugar
1 (3 inch) cinnamon stick
1 T. butter
1/2 t. ground cardamom
1 whole almond, shelled and blanched
1 T. ground cinnamon
1 to 2 c. half and half

Preheat oven to 325°. Butter a deep 2-quart casserole dish and set aside. In a medium saucepan, combine rice, salt, and boiling water. Cover and simmer over low heat for 10 minutes. Stir in whipping cream, milk, cinnamon stick, eggs, butter, 1/3 c. sugar, cardamom, and almond.

Spoon rice mixture into prepared dish. Bake 2 hours or until rice swells. In a small bowl, combine 1/2 c. sugar and 1 T. cinnamon. Serve hot or cold topped with half and half and cinnamon-sugar mix.

Créme Brulée with Pêches Flambées

Millie Dent   *France*

Makes 6 servings

Pêches Flambées:
1 large can peaches (or equivalent in fresh peaches)
Maple syrup
2 wine glasses brandy

Cold Créme Brulée:
4 eggs
1 1/2 pints heavy cream
pinch of salt
brown sugar, sifted

Pêches Flambées: Place peeled, drained peach halves (close together) in a shallow baking dish, adding maple syrup to almost cover fruit and heat thoroughly in oven. Brown under broiler for 1 minute. At the last minute, pour brandy over top, light, and bring flaming to the table.

Créme Brulée: Beat eggs together with cream and salt. Cook over hot water, stirring constantly until smooth and thick. When cool, pour into a lightly buttered shallow casserole. Chill thoroughly. Sprinkle top completely with a layer of sifted (no lumps) brown sugar. Run under broiler until sugar melts, and forms a crust. Be sure to watch carefully so that it does not burn. Chill in refrigerator several hours before serving.

Finskbrød (shortbread cookies)

Susanne M. Bromfield   Denmark

30 minutes to prepare; 10 minutes to bake

2 c. flour
1 c. butter
1/2 c. sugar
1 egg white, beaten
almonds, finely chopped
1/2 c. sugar

Cut the butter into the flour and sugar on a board or counter top. Gather into a ball, as one would for pie crust. Roll the soft dough into 1/2 inch thick lengths, about 2 inches wide. Cut these lengths into 1-inch pieces. Press each piece first into the egg white, the chopped nuts, and lastly the sugar. Place on greased waxed paper or cookie sheet and bake in a 400° oven for 10 minutes, or until lightly browned. Remove to rack and cool completely. Store in an airtight container.

Carrot Cake

Wendy

About 1 hour to prepare

2 c. sugar
4 eggs
1 1/3 c. oil
2 c. pre-sifted flour
2 t. baking soda
2 t. baking powder
2 t. cinnamon
4 c. grated carrots
3/4 c. broken nuts
3/4 c. raisins (optional)
cream cheese frosting

Preheat oven to 350°. Grease and flour a loaf pan. Beat sugar and eggs till thickened, and stir in oil. Sift together flour, baking soda, powder, and cinnamon. Stir into egg mixture. Fold in carrots, nuts, and raisins. Spoon into pan. Bake for 35 minutes. Cool. Top with cream cheese frosting.

Cream Cheese Frosting

1 pkg. (8oz.) cream cheese
1/2 c. margarine
1 t. vanilla
1 lb. confectioners sugar, sifted

Beat all ingredients together until well blended and velvety. Put on carrot cake.

Cheese Cake

Norma Weiss   *Italy*

Makes 12-16 servings

crust:
2 c. crushed cinnamon crisp
1/4 lb. melted butter
1/3 c. sugar

filling:
5 pkg. (8 oz.) cream cheese, softened
4 eggs
1 1/2 c. sugar
2 egg yolks
3 T. flour
1/2 c. heavy cream
1 T. orange juice
1 T. lemon juice
1/4 t. vanilla

glaze:
16 oz. frozen berries
2 T. cornstarch

To the crushed cinnamon crisp, add melted butter and sugar. Press mixture onto the bottom and sides of a well greased 9" spring form pan.

Preheat oven to 500°. Combine cream cheese, sugar, flour, juices, and vanilla. Beat with an electric blender. Beat in eggs and yolks, one at a time. Add heavy cream. Beat until well blended. Pour into prepared crumbs. Bake for 10 minutes at 500°, then reduce heat to 250° and bake for an additional one hour and twenty minutes. Let stand one hour. Refrigerate for at least six hours before serving.

After cooling, thaw berries. Put syrup from berries in a sauce pan, and add cornstarch. Heat and stir until thick. Let cool. Add fruit Glaze top of cake.

Espresso Pie

Lela Rotondo   *Italy*

15 minutes to prepare; chill overnight

2 15 oz. containers of ricotta cheese
2 half pints heavy cream, whipped
1/2 c. sugar
1 c. espresso coffee
1 t. vanilla
2 T. slivered almonds
1 1/2 T. gelatin
3 T. cold water
1 graham cracker pie crust
graham cracker crumbs

Sprinkle gelatin over cold water and stir. Add sugar and warm espresso and allow to cool. Stir in ricotta and vanilla and fold in whipped cream. Pour half of mixture into crust. Layer with graham cracker crumbs. Pour in the rest of mixture. Top with almonds if desired. Chill overnight.

Vasilopeta (New Year's Cake)

Greece

12 c. flour
1 c. butter
1 1/2 c. sugar
6 eggs
1 c. milk
1 t. anise flavor
2 pkgs. dry yeast
1 t. salt
grated lemon or orange rind

Dissolve yeast in a bowl with one cup of warm water. Add enough flour to make a thick batter. Cover bowl with a napkin, and set aside in a warm place to rise for one hour.

Place remaining flour in a large bowl, make a lake in the center and pour in the batter. Rinse the bowl that contained the batter with warm milk and add to the flour. Add remaining ingredients, putting one egg yolk aside for glazing. Knead for about 10 minutes, until smooth. Make a hard dough, cover dough, and set aside in a warm place to rise (about 2-3 hours or until doubled in bulk). Turn on a floured board and knead like a loaf of bread. Shape by hand in a well-greased baking pan. Leave enough space in the pan for rising. The dough should be about 1 1/2 inches thick. Make a small cut in the dough and insert a foil wrapped coin. Smooth over the dough so that the cut can not be seen.

Beat the reserved egg yolk with a little water and brush the surface with glaze. Bake in moderate oven for about one hour until brown.

No-Cook Chocolate Oatmeal Cookies

Linda Huss

Makes 6-7 dozen cookies

1/4 c. cocoa
1 stick butter
2 c. sugar
1/2 c. milk
2 t. vanilla
1 t. salt
1/2 c. crunchy peanut butter
4 c. quick oatmeal

Melt cocoa, butter, sugar and milk over direct heat. Bring to a boil, then remove from heat.

Add vanilla, salt, peanut butter, and oatmeal. Mix thoroughly and quickly. Drop by teaspoon on waxed paper.

Time permitting, heat oatmeal for 10 minutes in a 300° oven on a cookie sheet to brown a bit, before adding to mix. This improves the flavor of the cookies but is not necessary.

Best Crumb Cake

Marianna Rotondo

40 minutes to prepare

1 box yellow cake mix
2 1/2 c. flour
1/2 c. sugar
2 or 3 t. cinnamon
2 sticks melted margarine
confectionery sugar

Prepare yellow cake as directed on box. Cook for 15 minutes at 350° in a 9" x 13" pan.

While cake is baking, make the crumbs by mixing together the flour, sugar, cinnamon, and margarine. Take the cake out after 15 minutes and sprinkle the blended crumb mixture on top.

Put cake back in oven for about 25 minutes until done. Remove from oven and sprinkle confectionery sugar on top when cool.

Easy and Best Cheese Cake

Marianna Rotondo

graham crucker crust
2 8 oz. pkgs. cream cheese
1 pint sour cream
3 eggs
1 c. sugar
1 t. vanilla

Make or buy graham cracker crust. Use a springform pan.

Mix all remaining ingredients with a spoon (allow cream cheese and eggs to remain at room temperature an hour before mixing). Beat with beater at medium speed until light and fluffy.

Pour into graham cracker crust and bake for 30 minutes at 350°. Then, turn off heat and leave cake in oven for 1 more hour. Let cool completely. Refrigerate.

Hamantaschen

(Purim Cookies for the 14th day of Adar)

The Griffel Family

40 minutes to bake

2 c. sifted flour
1 1/2 t. baking powder
1/2 t. salt
2 eggs
1/2 c. melted margarine
1/2 c. sugar
1 t. lemon juice
1 can poppy seed filling

Beat eggs and margarine, then add sugar and lemon juice. Separately combine flour, baking soda, and salt. Add together. Work until dough is formed.

Place on a board and roll until 1/4" thick. Cut with cookie cutter to form round pieces of dough. Place approximately 2 T. of poppy seed filling in the center of each cookie. Turn up edges of round cookie to form three corners. Pinch the edges together.

Brush the cookies with melted margarine mixture. Bake at 375° for 35 to 40 minutes.

Poor Man's Cake

Melissa Napolitano

40-55 minutes to bake

4 c. sifted flour
2 c. sugar
1 T. cocoa
2-3 t. cinnamon
2-3 t. clover
2-3 t. allspice
1/2 t. salt
1 box raisins (15 oz.)
1 c. coarsely chopped walnuts
1 c. coffee
1/2 c. oil
1 t. baking soda

Cook raisins in 2 1/2 c. of boiling water for 5 minutes. Cool. Place all dry ingredients (except baking soda and coffee) into a large bowl. When raisins are cool, add coffee, oil and baking soda to raisins and stir quickly. Pour into dry ingredients and mix well.

Pour mixture into a greased and floured roasting pan (10" x 14" x 2"). Preheat oven to 450° and bake for 10 minutes. Reduce heat to 350° and bake for another 30-45 minutes.

Anise Cookies

Caron Kass   *Italy*

Makes 4 dozen cookies
Bakes 65 minutes

1/2 c. butter, softened
1 1/3 c. granulated sugar
1/2 t. salt
finely grated zest of 1 medium orange
finely grated zest of 1 medium lemon
1 T. anise seeds
3 eggs
3 c. all-purpose flour
2 1/2 t. baking powder
1/2 t. baking soda
2 c. sliced toasted almonds, coarsely chopped

Preheat oven to 325°. Generously grease 2 large baking sheets. In a large mixing bowl beat butter, sugar, salt, orange zest, lemon zest, and anise seeds until light. Add eggs, one at a time, beating well after each addition. Stir in flour, baking powder, baking soda, and nuts.

Divide dough into thirds. With buttered fingers, shape each portion of dough into a log about 12" long and 1 1/2" in diameter. Place two logs 4" apart on one baking sheet and the other log on the other baking sheet. Using your palms, flatten the logs slightly to about 1" thickness. Bake 25 minutes, rotating baking sheets from top to bottom midway through baking.

Remove cookies from oven. Reduce heat to 275°. Using a thin-bladed knife, cut rolls at a 45° angle into 3/4" slices. Lay slices cut side down, 1 1/2" apart on cookie sheets. Bake an additional 40 minutes, or until very dry.

Cool cookies on rack, and store in an air-tight container.

Pavlova Cake
(a meringue confection)

New Zealand

1 1/2 hours to bake

4 egg whites
1 c. sugar
1 t. vinegar
1/2 t. vanilla
pinch of salt

Beat egg whites until stiff. Add sugar gradually.
   Then fold in vanilla and vinegar. Bake in a very slow oven for 1 1/2 hours. Fill with whipped cream and fruit.

The Ronald McDonald House of NYC is a temporary home to pediatric cancer patients and their families from all over the world.

Cheesecake

Dyan Sayles

One hour to bake; leave in unopened oven for one more hour

graham cracker crust
2 c. graham cracker crumbs
1 stick butter, melted
2 T. cinnamon
1 t. nutmeg
1/4 c. sugar
3-8oz. cream cheese
1 pint sour cream
1/2 pint heavy cream
4 eggs
1 1/2 c. sugar
1 t. vanilla

Butter sides and bottom of springform pan. Combine first six ingredients and press into pan. Save 1/2 c. of mixture for topping.

Soften cream cheese to room temperature. Add eggs and blend with cream cheese. Add sour cream and heavy cream and blend until soft. Add sugar and vanilla. Mix all together for ten minutes. Pour into prepared crust.

Bake for 1 hour. Turn off oven and leave in oven for one more hour. DO NOT OPEN THE OVEN DOOR. After that, remove from the oven and let cool. Refrigerate for several hours or overnight. Top with 1/2 c. mixture of crumbs.

Gran Pecan Pie

Dyan Sayles

45-50 minutes to bake

1 pastry shell, chilled
3 eggs, at room temperature
2 T. melted butter
1 c. sugar
1/2 t. salt
1 c. dark corn syrup
1 t. vanilla
1 c. pecans, coarsely chopped
1 c. pecan halves
1/2 c. Gran Marnier

Make pastry shell. Preheat oven to 400°. Combine eggs, sugar, salt, corn syrup, Gran Marnier, butter and vanilla in a medium bowl. Beat with electric mixer until well blended. Setting aside 10 pecan halves, stir pecans into mixture. Pour into chilled pie crust. In the center of the pie, make a little design with the 10 pecan halves.

Place on lowest oven rack and bake for 15 minutes at 400°. Reduce oven temperature to 350° and bake for 30-35 minutes or until crust is lightly browned and filling is set. Serve at room temperature with whipped cream.

Cherry Nut Crumble

Wini Cudjoe   *England*

Makes 6 servings

15 minutes to prepare, 30 minutes to cook

1 oz. caster sugar
1/2 oz. corn flour
1 1/2 lb. cherries, stoned
juice of 1 orange

For the crumble:
6 oz. plain flour
3 oz. butter, cut into cubes
1/2 t. ground nutmeg
2 oz. dark, soft brown sugar
2 oz. blanched almonds, chopped

Butter a 2-pint oven proof dish. Preheat oven to 400°. Mix together sugar and corn flour. Toss cherries in mixture, then heat gently in a pan until juices start to run. Add remaining sugar mix and orange juice and heat, stirring until thickened. Spoon into a dish.

Sift flour in a bowl. Add butter and rub in until mixture resembles fine bread crumbs. Stir in nutmeg, sugar and almonds.

Spoon crumble over fruit. Cook for 25-30 minutes until topping is crisp and golden. Serve hot or cold with custard or cream.

Meringues

Andew Nawn's Mom

25 minutes to bake

2 egg whites
1/8 t. cream of tartar
1/8 t. salt
1 t. vanilla
3/4 c. sugar
6 oz. tiny chocolate bits
1/2 c. walnuts, chopped

Beat together first four ingredients. Add sugar gradually. Beat until firm peaks form. Add chocolate bits and walnuts. Drop onto greased cookie sheet. Bake at 300° for 25 minutes

Cape Cod Cranberry Pie

Andrew Nawn's Mom   *United States*

One hour to bake

2 c. cranberries
1 c. white sugar
1/2 c. walnuts, chopped
1 extra large egg, beaten well
1/2 c. brown sugar
1 c. flour
1/2 c. melted butter
1/2 t. cinnamon

Place cranberries, 1/2 c. white sugar, and walnuts in a greased 10" pie plate. Separately combine remaining sugars and egg. Gradually add flour, butter, and cinnamon. Pour on top of cranberries. Bake for one hour at 350°. Serve with ice cream.

Plymouth Plantation Indian Pudding

Andrew Nawn's Mom

30 minutes to bake

1 quart milk
4 T. yellow cornmeal
1/2 c. molasses
1/2 c. sugar
1 t. cinnamon
1 t. ginger
1/2 t. salt
1/2-1 c. raisins (optional)
2 eggs
2 T. butter

Scald milk, add cornmeal. Stir and cook for 10 minutes.

In a greased baking dish, combine molasses, sugar, cinnamon, ginger, salt, and raisins. Add milk and cornmeal mixture slowly. Stir in beaten eggs and butter. Place dish in a large pan of hot water in 350° oven. Bake for 30 minutes or until knife inserted in the center comes out clean. Serve warm with ice cream or whipped cream.

Chocolate Truffle

Jackie Russell

chocolate cake mix
3 pkgs. chocolate pudding/pie mix
whipped cream
3 Skor candy bars

Prepare and bake chocolate cake and pudding according to package directions. After cake has cooled, cut the cake into small squares and arrange 1 layer on the bottom of a truffle or deep dish. Then scoop on a layer of chocolate pudding. Then add a layer of whipped cream. Repeat the layering until all are used up. You should end with the whipped cream. Top with crushed Skor candy bars. Chill and set before serving.

Noodle Pudding

Amy Resnikoff

Makes 6-8 servings
1 hour and 15 minutes to prepare

1 lb. box of noodles
1 8 oz. can crushed pineapple
1/2 lb. cottage cheese
1 c. (8 oz.) sour cream
1/2 c. brown sugar
3 eggs
3 T. sugar
1 t. vanilla
5 T. + 2 tsp. butter or margarine
1/2 cup raisins
1 t. cinnamon
1/4 c. graham cracker crumbs

Pre-heat oven to 350°. Put pineapple and 2 T. sugar in a small pot. Cover and cook for 1 minute. Remove from heat. Cook noodles for 5 minutes and rinse with water.

Take cottage cheese, 4 T. butter, brown sugar, egg, sour cream, vanilla and mix in a blender. Add noodles and pineapple. Spill off juice. Add raisins.

Pour mixture into greased baking dish. Separately blend graham cracker crumbs, cinnamon, 1 T. sugar. Pour over top of mixture. Put slivers of butter on top. Bake for 1 hour.

Breads, Sauces, & Other Goodies

Suzanne's Kitchen Meat Sauce

Suzanne Birnbaum

30 minutes to prepare

1 lb. ground beef
onions
garlic
12 oz. can tomato paste
15 oz. can tomato sauce
water
salt and pepper to taste

In a pan, with salt, simmer ground beef until brown with a little onion and garlic. Drain the grease. Add tomato paste, 1 can water, and tomato sauce. Simmer for 20 minutes. Serve over pasta.

Shrimp Cocktail Sauce

Hilda Franck

15 minutes to prepare

1 c. mayonnaise
1/4 c. chili sauce
1 t. tomato puree
lemon juice
tabasco sauce
1/4 c. whipped cream
1 t. gin

To one cup mayonnaise, add 1/4 c. of chili sauce, one t. tomato puree, a little lemon juice, and a few drops of tabasco sauce. Then add 1/4 cup of whipped cream and one teaspoon of gin. Mix well.

Vit Sås (White Sauce)

Nordic Delicacies Inc.   *Sweden*

Makes 2 cups

1/4 c. butter
1/4 c. all-purpose flour
1 1/2 c. milk
1 t. salt
1/4 t. ground all-spice or white pepper

Melt butter in medium saucepan over medium heat. Stir in flour. Slowly stir in milk.

Stirring constantly, cook until sauce is thickened and smooth. Stir in salt and all-spice or white pepper. Serve hot.

Joanne's Butterscotch Sauce

Andrew Nawn's Mom

One hour to cook

2 1/2 c. sugar
1 1/2 c. white Karo syrup
1 c. milk
1 c. cream
2 T. butter
dash of salt
1 t. vanilla

Simmer all ingredients except vanilla slowly, stirring for 1 hour. Add vanilla. Pour into jars while warm.

Mrs. Bailey's Fudge Sauce

Andrew Nawn's Mom   *USA*

20 minutes to prepare
Makes 1 quart

3/4 stick butter or margarine
4 squares unsweetened chocolate
2 T. dutch cocoa
3 c. confectioner's sugar (1 lb. box)
1 can evaporated milk
1 t. salt
1 t. vanilla

Melt butter or margarine in double boiler. Add unsweetened chocolate. When melted, add cocoa. Add confectioners sugar, alternating with evaporated milk. Keep stirring these into mixture until well blended and smooth. Add salt. Cook for 5 minutes or until sauce begins to thicken. Remove from heat and add vanilla.

Pour into jars while still lukewarm, as it hardens when cool.

Mumma (beer punch)

Nordic Delicacies Inc.   *Sweden*

Makes 6 servings

1 12 oz. bottle dark beer
1 12 oz. bottle light beer
1 12 oz. bottle pale ale
1/4 c. aquavit or gin

Refrigerate all ingredients until thoroughly chilled. To serve pour all ingredients into a chilled pitcher; stir. Serve in mugs.

Elegant Shrimp Sauce for Pasta

Andrew Nawn's Mom

30 minutes to cook

1 lb. medium shrimp
1 large onion, chopped
2 cloves garlic, minced
5-6 scallions, green part only, chopped
1/2 t. oregano
4 T. olive oil
1 medium head broccoli, cut into florets
1 (35 oz.) can tomatoes, chopped and partially drained
1/2 t. basil

Heat olive oil in a large skillet. Sauté onions, scallions, and garlic until onions are transparent. Add broccoli and sauté for 2 minutes. Add tomatoes and seasonings and cook for 15 minutes. Add shrimp and cook 5-10 minutes longer. Serve over cooked pasta.

A Very Versatile Marinade

Diana Dent McGraw   *United States*

5 minutes to prepare

1 T. fresh ginger
1 clove garlic
1 t. brown sugar
1 T. reduced sodium soy sauce
1 t. ground coriander

Mix all ingredients together. Great with lamb, pork, or beef. It penetrates the meat quickly and adds a lot of flavor!

Old Fashioned Northern Italian Pasta Sauce

Beth Shubert's grandmother   *Northern Italy*

Makes 6-10 servings
2-3 hours to prepare

1 (28 oz.) can of peeled and crushed tomatoes
2 (18 oz.) cans tomato sauce
1 (8 oz.) can tomato paste
1 stick of salted butter
1 small bunch fresh parsley, finely chopped
3 sprigs fresh basil, or 1 T. dried basil, chopped
3 large cloves garlic, minced
1 medium onion, chopped
3 bay leaves
1/4 c. dried Italian Porcini mushrooms, soaked in hot water
   for 10 minutes, and chopped after rehydrated
1 T. salt
1 t. pepper
1 T. sugar (optional)
1/2 c. of good olive oil
1/2 c. red wine
2 c. water

Let olive oil heat in large, deep pot. Add garlic and stir. Add onion, lower heat to medium, and let onion and garlic brown slightly. Do not burn garlic. Add parsley, basil, bay leaves, butter, and mushrooms. Sauté 2-3 minutes until butter melts. Add salt and pepper, tomato paste, and tomato sauce. Stir and let simmer 2-3 minutes.

Add tomatoes, simmer 2-3 minutes. Add wine, sugar, and water and let simmer, stirring well. Reduce heat so that only tiny bubbles gently rise to the surface of the sauce; sauce should not be boiling heavily. Let simmer, stirring every 10 minutes and scraping sauce on top sides of pot into sauce, for 1 1/2 to 2 hours until thickened. Freezes well once cooled.

Matzoh Balls

Jane Birnbaum

Makes 4-6 servings

2 eggs, separated
1 T. chicken fat
pinch of nutmeg
1 onion, grated
Matzoh meal

Mix chicken fat into egg yolks. Grate onion into yolks. Stir in nutmeg. Sprinkle in matzoh meal and stir until firm. In a separate bowl, beat egg whites until stiff. Refrigerate each bowl. Then fold beaten egg whites into egg yolk mixture. Add more matzoh meal as needed to keep mixture stiff. Boil a large pot of water. Using a tablespoon and wet hands, make small matzoh balls out of mixture and drop into boiling water for 15-20 minutes. Lift out with slotted spoon and put into soup.

Egg Soufflé

Suzanne Birnbaum

6 eggs
2 c. milk
8 slices challah, trim crusts
1/8 stick butter, melted
8 oz. grated sharp cheddar cheese
salt and pepper

Grease a 9" x 11" pan. Cut bread into cubes. Make alternate layers of bread and cheese. In a separate bowl, mix eggs well; add milk, salt and pepper. Pour over the bread and cheese, then pour melted butter over top. Refrigerate if not using right away. Take out 1 1/2 hours before cooking. Bake at 350° for 1 hour.

Swedish Pancakes

Nordic Delicacies Inc.   *Sweden*

Makes 20 pancakes

1 egg
3/4 c. milk
1/4 t. salt
1/2 c. all-purpose flour
1 t. baking powder
1 T. sugar
2 T. butter, melted
Lingonberries
dairy sour cream

Preheat plater pan (cast-iron Swedish pan with shallow, round indentations for making thin pancakes about 3 inches in diameter).

In a large bowl, beat egg; stir in milk, salt, flour, baking powder, and sugar until batter is smooth. Stir in melted butter. Grease cups in hot pan with shortening or butter. Spoon 2 rounded tablespoons batter into each greased cup. Cook about 1 minute on each side, or until golden brown. Serve immediately with lingonberries and sour cream.

Breakfast Snack

Ruth Lynch   *United States*

Makes 8 to 10 servings
35 minutes to bake

12 eggs
1 lb. cheddar cheese, shredded
1 lb. Monterey Jack cheese, shredded
1 (4-oz.) jar salsa

Beat eggs in bowl. Add cheeses and salsa; mix well. Pour into ungreased 9" x 13" baking dish. Bake at 350° for 35 minutes.

Serve warm or cold with muffins and fruit.

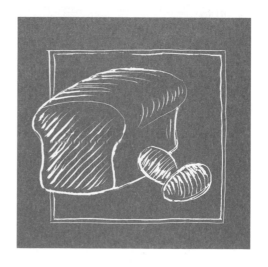

Mandel Bread

Marcia Potash

10-15 minutes to bake; 5 minutes to cool; 5-10 minutes to toast

1 3/4 c. flour
1 t. baking powder
1 pinch salt
2 eggs
1/2 c. sugar
1/2 c. vegetable oil
1 t. vanilla
optional: chocolate chips and chopped walnuts

Preheat oven to 350°. Combine dry ingredients in small mixing bowl. In a large mixing bowl, beat eggs and add sugar. Keep stirring and add oil and vanilla. Add flour mixture a little at a time. Then add optional ingredients, if desired.

Form very moist mixture in 3 loaves on one cookie sheet. Bake for 10-15 minutes or until golden. Cool for 5 minutes. Slice the loaves into 8-11 slices each. Turn the slices on their sides and toast for 5-10 minutes.

Zucchini Bread

Aunt Vicki

1 hour, 45 minutes to prepare

1 lb. zucchini
salt
2 3/4 c. flour
1 1/2 t. baking powder
1 t. baking soda
1/2 t. cinnamon
3 eggs
1 c. sugar
1/2 c. vegetable oil or softened margarine
rind of lemon, grated
1 T. lemon juice
1 t. vanilla extract
1 c. walnuts, chopped (optional)

Wash, trim and coarsely grate zucchini. Salt and let stand for 30 minutes, then drain and squeeze dry. Sift together the flour, baking powder, baking soda, cinnamon, and 1/2 t. salt. Set aside. Beat together the eggs, sugar, and oil. Mix in the lemon juice, lemon rind, and vanilla. Beat in the dry ingredients and stir in the zucchini. Add the nuts if you wish. Pour into a greased and floured 9x5" loaf pan, and bake in a pre-heated oven at 350° for 50-60 minutes.

Challah

Esther Berkowitz   *Polish-Jewish*

Makes an extra-large loaf
Leave plenty of time to prepare, 1 1/2 hours to bake

4 lbs. flour
2 pkgs. cake yeast
6 oz. oil
4-6 oz. sugar (depending on desired sweetness)
1/2 t. salt
6 eggs

Place 6 cups of flour into a large bowl. Make a hole in the middle.

Crumble both cakes of yeast into an 8 oz. glass of warm water. Mix well with a spoon until the yeast is dissolved.

Pour into hole in the flour. Mix with a wooden spoon. Add oil, sugar, and salt. Mix.

Add 5 egg yolks and 6 egg whites. Reserve the sixth egg yolk. Mix thoroughly with a wooden spoon.

Add more flour as needed until mixture is no longer sticky.

Knead for at least 5 minutes. Smooth dough into a ball. Leave in bowl. Let stand, covered with a cloth in a warm place until dough rises at least double in size (2-3 hours).

After first rise, knead again and let stand covered until risen (about 2 hours).

Shape into desired shape on a floured board. Can braid if divided into three parts and rolled into long strands. Then fold over on one another. Mix the left-over sixth egg yolk with one teaspoon water. Brush on top and sides of challah. Let rise for about an hour on a pan that has been prepared with wax paper and a bit of oil. Pan can be a cookie sheet or a 9" x 12" baking pan.

Put into 325° oven and bake approximately 1 1/2 hours until golden brown.

Brown Soda Bread

Eileen Moore   *Ireland*

Makes 20 servings
50 minutes to bake

6 c. white bleached flour
4 c. whole wheat flour
1 t. baking soda
1 t. salt
1 egg
1 carton buttermilk
1 t. baking powder

Mix together flours, baking soda, baking powder, and salt in a large bowl.

Whisk up buttermilk and egg. Add buttermilk mixture to flour mixture and mix. Add extra flour to make a dry mixture if needed.

Knead for about 5 minutes. Shape into a round loaf shape, and make a criss-cross design with a knife.

Put on a floured baking tray and place in a preheated oven for 50 minutes at 350°.

Apple Cinnamon Bread

Fran Sharp   *United States*

40-50 minutes to bake

2 c. chopped apples
2 T. lemon juice
1/2 c. light brown sugar
4 T. melted butter
1 egg
1 c. unbleached flour
1 c. whole wheat flour
2 t. baking powder
1/2 t. baking soda
pinch salt
2 t. cinnamon
1 T. vanilla extract

Combine apple and lemon juice. Cream together sugar, butter, and egg. Add this to the chopped apples. Sift dry ingredients in a bowl. Add wet mixture and vanilla to dry ingredients. Mix well. Bake in a buttered and floured loaf pan at 350° for 40-50 minutes.

Banana Pecan Bread

Caron Kass

1 hour to bake; 10 minutes to cool

1/2 c. (1 stick) butter
1 c. granulated sugar
2 large egg whites
1 t. vanilla extract
3 ripe bananas
2 c. all-purpose flour
1 1/2 t. baking soda
2 t. ground cinnamon
1/2 t. salt
1 c. buttermilk
1 c. chopped pecans
4-6 pecan halves

Preheat oven to 350°. Generously grease and flour a large loaf pan (9" x 5").

In a large bowl, cream together butter and sugar until light and fluffy. Add eggs, one at a time. Then add vanilla. Mash bananas to a puree, add to the previous mixture, and beat with a wooden spoon. Sift together dry ingredients, and add to banana mixture, while also adding buttermilk. Stir well, and then add the chopped pecans.

Arrange pecan halves on the bottom of the loaf pan and pour in batter gently, so as not to move the pecans. Bake for an hour or until tester inserted in the center comes out clean. Let cool for 10 minutes in the pan, and then remove gently from the pan and let cool completely on a rack.